THE HUBERT H. HUMPHREY
METRODOME
SOUVENIR BOOK

A Pictorial History of the Twins, Vikings, Gophers, Millers, Saints — and Metrodome!

Compiled by Dave Mona

MSP Publications, Inc.
Minneapolis, Minnesota

Printed in the United States of America

ISBN 0-9607982-0-X

Cover Illustration by Mike Reed.

Corner action cartoon by Jack Molloy.

MSP Publications, Inc.
512 Nicollet Mall, Suite 400
Minneapolis, MN 55402

Contents

Foreword

by MURIEL HUMPHREY BROWN

Hubert Humphrey was a man of many loves. He loved politics. He loved his state. He loved his family. *And* he loved sports: Hubert loved the competition; the crowds; the enthusiasm. There was nothing he enjoyed more than to sit in a crowd of fans, waiting for the kickoff or the opening pitch. He would never miss going to a Twins baseball game or a Vikings football game if he had a chance, no matter where they were playing. He would check regularly to see how his favorite teams were doing.

Hubert was thrilled by the prospect of having the Metrodome named after him. It wasn't vanity, because there were lots of other places which bore his name and he had a record of public service that was a lasting memorial. He was content with all that.

The Metrodome was different. He could see, in his mind, cheering crowds filled with excitement and pleasure. Their pleasure, their joy, week after week, year after year into the distant future, gave him great satisfaction. He would mimic Howard Cosell saying, "We are here at the Hubert H. Humphrey Memorial Stadium," and then laugh heartily. He liked the thought of it and the way it sounded.

When Hubert first came to the University of Minnesota, he became a Gopher fan. That was back in the days of the championship teams of that great coach, Bernie Bierman. And in our early years as mayor of Minneapolis, I remember attending many Millers games at Nicollet Park. And I remember, too, how Hubert rode throughout the state on a bus with the team in an effort to get rural as well as urban people more involved in supporting our professional athletes. Years later he would arrange air travel around the Vikings schedule, keep a governor (or all of us) waiting while he went to the locker room after a game to offer congratulations or do post-game analyses with the players. A political speech before cheering admirers barely brought the satisfaction of sitting with

Top: Humphrey with Calvin Griffith; bottom: Twins Manager Sam Mele, Baseball Commissioner Ford Frick and Los Angeles Manager Walt Alston watch the Vice President toss out the first ball of the 1965 World Series.

*To Alan Page—
all man—all champion
with admiration and
friendship
Hubert H. Humphrey*

Halsey Hall in the radio booth doing the play-by-play of a Twins game. Every pop fly looked to Hubert like it was going out of the park, his enthusiasm exceeding his eyesight in his desire that his team win.

There were a good many times when the players would return the enthusiasm and loyalty that Hubert had for them. I'll never forget the campaign team of Jim Marshall, Carl Eller and Alan Page who devoted so much of their precious time to help us in the primaries in 1972 and their help again in 1976. And, when Hubert was in the hospital at Sloan-Kettering in New York during the fall of 1976, the Vikings football games were so important to him. When they beat the Chicago Bears, the team sent him the game ball. I think that was one of the things that gave him the most encouragement to carry on during the months of struggle which followed.

Hubert would be so pleased that the great team spirit which has characterized sports throughout our state has been exemplified in the building of this magnificent stadium. The community faced a tough decision as to whether to build, or where to build, a stadium. But once the decision had been made, everyone pitched in—public and private sectors, business and labor—even those who had lost in the decision. Once again, community spirit— people working together—teamwork brought about tremendous achievement.

Hubert would have loved to be here for the first cheers in this impressive sports arena—his exuberant laughter and unmistakable voice joining ours. For the Humphrey family, and we hope for the people of Minnesota, those cheers will always remind us of a good man who loved us all.

Thank you for honoring him.

Alan Page, left, and Carl Eller were members of the Vikings' Purple People Eaters defense when they campaigned for Hubert Humphrey in 1972.

Metrodome Facts and Figures

QUESTION: How big is the scoreboard and does it have any special features?
The scoreboard is 164 feet long and 17 feet high. It features animation as well as instant replays.

QUESTION: How does a person write or call the Metrodome?
The Metrodome's official address is 900 South 5th Street, Minneapolis, Minnesota 55415. Its telephone number is (612) 332-0386.

QUESTION: How many on-site parking places are there?
For the general public there are no on-site parking places. The lot adjacent to the building has approximately 450 spaces. During events, 100 spaces are made available to the group holding the event. The remainder of the spaces are planned for charter buses.

QUESTION: Approximately how many people could be accommodated in the Metrodome for a concert or religious crusade?
The absolute capacity of the Metrodome for such an event is in the neighborhood of 72,000.

QUESTION: How many public restrooms are there in the Metrodome?
Thirty-two.

QUESTION: How many rows of seating are there in the upper and lower decks?
The upper deck has 32 rows of seating and the lower deck has 33 rows.

QUESTION: How big is the dome area itself?
The total dome area is 415,000 square feet, or 9.5 acres.

QUESTION: How far above the playing field is the dome when it is both inflated and deflated?
When inflated, the dome rises to 186 feet above the field. When deflated, the dome rests on cables 76 feet above the playing surface.

QUESTION: How many fans are used to keep the dome inflated?
The stadium is equipped with twenty 90-horsepower fans to keep the dome in place, although fewer than half are generally needed under normal conditions.

QUESTION: How much dirt was taken out and how many tons of steel were used?
Approximately 600,000 cubic yards of excavation, 300,000 cubic yards of backfill, 500 tons of structural steel and 40,000 cubic yards of concrete were used in the project.

QUESTION: Would it be possible for a baseball in play to come into contact with obstructions hanging from the roof?
The best targets will be the speakers suspended from the dome in right field. Ground rules will be established to cover balls hitting the speakers, but it is assumed that the ball will be in play as it falls off the speakers.

QUESTION: How high is the wall in right field?
The wall itself rises 40 feet above the playing field. There is a seven-foot-high fence in front of the wall, and any ball hitting the wall in fair territory will be a home run.

QUESTION: Which dugout do the Twins occupy and will the Vikings and their opponents still be on the same side of the field?
The Twins, who occupied the first-base dugout at Met Stadium, have moved to the third-base dugout at the Metrodome. It is assumed that the Vikings will have the bench on the east side of the field, nearest their locker room, and that the opponents will line up on the west side of the field.

QUESTION: How does the distance from the sidelines of the football field to the nearest seats compare to that of Met Stadium?
The distance from the front row of seats to the field is 60 feet. That compares with 100 or 120 feet from the closest sidelines' seats to the Met Stadium field.

QUESTION: In case it were necessary to play a baseball game in the morning and a football game at night, how long would it take to change from a baseball to a football configuration?
Although it remains to be tested, stadium officials estimate the change can be made in as little as four hours.

QUESTION: How does the size of the dome itself compare with other domes in the United States?
The Metrodome, at 9.5 acres, is the same size as the Houston Astrodome. Pontiac's Silverdome is slightly larger, at 10 acres, and New Orleans' Superdome is right behind at 9.7 acres. Seattle's King Dome is 7.4 acres.

QUESTION: How much would it cost to rent the Metrodome for an event?
If you want a unique way to entertain your friends, or are looking for an unusual spot to hold your wedding reception, the dome can be yours for as little as $20,000 plus event expenses.

QUESTION: How do they get rid of the pitchers' mound when they want to go to the football configuration?
The mound can be lowered hydraulically to a position beneath the playing field. This option, however, will not be available to managers wishing to send starting pitchers to an early shower.

HUBERT H. HUMPHREY METRODOME

OWNER:
Metropolitan Sports Facilities Commission
Chairman: Dan Brutger
Executive Director: Don Poss
CONSTRUCTION MANAGER:
Barton-Malow/Construction
Management Services, Inc.
ARCHITECT:
Skidmore, Owings & Merrill, Chicago
CONSTRUCTION START:
December 1979
DOME INFLATION: October 2, 1981
COMPLETION:
March 1982
SEATING CAPACITY:
62,500/football
54,791/baseball
OVERALL DIMENSIONS:
727 ft. × 612 ft. × 189 feet high
FIELD ELEVATION:
48 ft. below existing grade
FULL SITE:
20 acres

The Long Road to the Metrodome

by DICK SCHAAF

Ground for the Metrodome was figuratively broken in the late 1960s when Minneapolis architect Robert G. Cerny began talking up the idea of a domed football stadium to be located somewhere in the downtown area. No one could have predicted then that the quest to build a domed stadium would itself become a football to be kicked all over the Twin Cities political landscape.

For ten years the battle raged across the gridiron of business, media and especially politics—both local and state. There were public hearings and private planning sessions, closet votes and large-scale referendums, charges and counter-charges, deals supposedly made but never kept. And in the process there were proposals to dome virtually any existing structure that didn't move or protest, and plans to build stadiums almost everywhere except in the middle of Lake Minnetonka and at Sparky the Seal's tank at the Como Park Zoo.

The tale of the domes that didn't happen brings back names and places and faces perhaps better left undisturbed. The Third Avenue North Distributor. Lakeville's earth stadium. A dome for the state fairgrounds. One on Metropolitan Stadium, and one behind it. Doming Memorial Stadium at the University of Minnesota, and building a new one on the St. Paul campus. Domes in Eagan, and Coon Rapids, and Blaine, and on Midway Stadium. Not to mention the infamous Board of Equalization and Taxation.

It's a story of numbers. Seat numbers—57,000, 65,000, 71,000, 105,000. Dollar numbers—$10 million, $24 million, $49 million, $100 million. And it all began in 1975.

That was the year the Metropolitan Stadium leases for the Twins and the Vikings were due to expire. Unless something was done to provide at least the Vikings with a larger place in which to play, there was the very real

fear—made all the more vivid by the successful move of the Minneapolis Lakers basketball franchise to Los Angeles—that Minnesota sports fans would someday see the Twin Cities become "a very cold Omaha."

As far back as 1969, the Metropolitan Sports Area Commission (four members from Minneapolis, one each from Bloomington and Richfield) had gotten both teams to agree informally to a remodeling and expansion of the Met. This was designed primarily to satisfy the Vikings, then playing in the National Football League's smallest stadium, and one with poor sight lines which put only half the seats between the goal lines.

It seemed a simple enough proposition. When the Twins had arrived to begin playing at the Met in 1961, Minneapolis had floated the bonds which allowed the former home of the Minneapolis Millers to be enlarged for major league baseball. Now the same system was proposed again—let Minneapolis put up the money for refurbishing the Bloomington stadium. And right there the battle lines were clearly drawn along the border between the two cities. With speculative glances at their struggling downtown and the growing I-494 strip, a few members of the Minneapolis City Council and then-City Coordinator Tommy Thompson decided Cerny's dome-dreaming was worth investigating.

Even this early in the ball game there were other plans afoot. There was, for example, a 75,000-seat facility proposed as part of a 210-acre dome, hotel/motel, office and entertainment complex in Blaine—along with moving the airport to the Anoka area as well. And there was talk of doming Memorial Stadium at the U—talk only, given the cost and limited feasibility of reworking the nearly 60-year-old Brick House.

But mostly it was a tug-of-war between Bloomington and Minneapolis. Bloomington had several plans: from adding 10,000 seats and Viking offices at the Met to building a brand new facility behind the stadium, a 65,000-seat dome priced at a modest $10.5 million to be located along 24th Avenue S.

Minneapolis, alas, had no plan—yet. But plans are a lot cheaper than domes, and Cerny was soon fleshing out his cherished fantasy. It turned out to be a heck of a proposal.

The "didn't dome that almost did" was designed to fit into the northwest side of Hennepin Avenue between Seventh and Tenth Streets North and across First Avenue. Its 65,000 seats were to be hung inside a 5,100-space parking ramp (spaces circling up six miles from the lowest

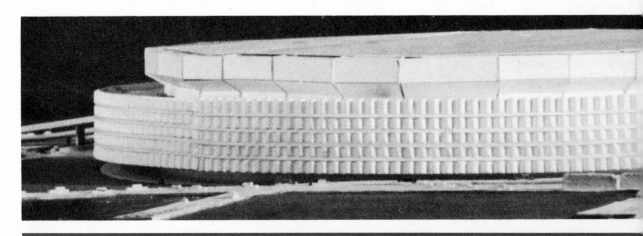

point, two stories underground, to the 440 slots at the top of the dome reserved for tailgaters). The 670-foot dome would be solid, not translucent; the field below laid out for football—and ultimately that newfangled European import, soccer—but not baseball. Nearly 60 percent of its seats would be between the goal lines, sight lines were guaranteed outstanding, a basketball complex could eventually be added and, when not in use for football, the dome could be rented by everything from horse shows to the Billy Graham Crusade.

There was more. The stadium itself would hang over the Third Avenue North Distributor connecting Hwy. 12 to Washington Avenue N. as part of the I-394 system. It would be linked to the downtown through the city's skyways, with the main corridor to cross Hennepin between Seventh and Eighth streets. Its parking spaces would be occupied weekdays by people working downtown, producing revenue even when football was out of season. (There were to be 48 traffic lines entering/exiting the dome, leading proponents to boast that a sellout crowd would clear the downtown in 30 minutes flat.)

What was all this going to cost? The first figure was $49.1 million for stadium and ramp (state and federal money would take care of the highway part of it), to be financed by general obligation bonds at a now-innocent 5 percent rate of interest. With speedy approval, promoters promised, the Vikings could kick-off the 1975 season under a roof.

And at that point, perhaps predictably, the roof fell in.

There were 200 people in the F&M Savings Bank auditorium Jan. 12, 1972, when the first report on the proposed dome was presented to the Downtown Council, which had co-funded it with the City Council. There were more than 800 at the raucous public hearing just about a year later when then-Mayor Charles Stenvig pledged to veto the dome proposal if the City Council sent it to him.

(This was the same Mayor Charles Stenvig, it should be noted, who a little more than a year before had confessed, "I'm excited about it. I'd love to see it come to downtown.")

The original proposed dome came to be seen as a heavy load about to be laid on the bowed back of the city's taxpayers. Its low cost estimates were doubted. Its potential benefits were dismissed. Its businessmen supporters were derided. It was perceived as a boondoggle, not a business development, despite protestations to the contrary. At one point, the city contemplated producing a one-hour telethon to explain the proposal, but that never went on the air. Amid the rhetoric and bombast, at least nine of the 13 members of the Minneapolis City Council would have to fly in the face of public opinion and the mayor's promised veto to gain approval. The council eventually said yes, by 10-3. And when Mayor Stenvig delivered the veto he'd pledged, the council overrode him by the same 10-3 margin, setting the stage for a bizarre climax no one could have foreseen.

Came now the moment for the obscure, unknown, mysterious and unappreciated Board of Equalization and Taxation. This seven-person body would have to approve the issuance of bonds for the dome, along with the city's other public works projects, for 1973. Its members reflected the divided community in more ways than one. The mayor held a seat. So did the city council. The school board also was represented. Five votes were needed to approve. Four "yes" votes were assured, two "nos" (one of them Stenvig's). The swing man was one Albert P. Hum, who some thought was the mayor's man. Cynics insisted that Stenvig was playing both ends against the middle—voting "no" to look like the taxpayers' white knight while preparing to deliver Hum's fifth vote in favor so the dome would be approved anyway. The vote was set for February 14 . . . until it was discovered that Albert P. Hum had moved to Golden Valley and thus was

Cerny's Third Avenue North stadium was to be ringed by a 5,100-space, ten-story parking ramp. The open-air tenth level was designed for tail-gating parties and offered a panoramic skyline view. Plans also called for a skyway connection to downtown.

Plans for keeping the snow out of the Met included geodesic, cable and air-supported roof designs.

ineligible to vote at all. He resigned the next day. It was up to the mayor to appoint a replacement. It was up to the city council to approve the appointment. Five unapproved nominees later, Stenvig announced the seat would not be filled.

From that came the Chamber of Commerce task force that ultimately took the funding issue to the state level. From that came the current Industry Square site. From that ultimately came the Hubert H. Humphrey Metrodome. Clearly the dome would be built downtown. It just took a long time to figure out where and when.

In the meantime, the dome-dreaming didn't end. Lest they be forgot, here are *some* of the other "didn't domes":

• **The Fairgrounds Dome**—St. Paul Mayor Lawrence Cohen proposed a $60 million, 80,000-seat dome and mass transit facility, to be used by the Vikings and Gophers, on the Minnesota State Fairgrounds in Falcon Heights.

• **The Lakeville Earth Stadium**—One of the most original candidates, this stadium didn't have a dome in its original incarnation. It did have the most detailed seating figures, 65,925 (with potential to expand to 105,000), and the most novel design—excavated, with all seats below ground level a la the stadium on the University of Michigan campus. Its $26 million price tag was to be paid by up to 16,000 season ticketholders who would buy bonds priced from $1,500 for a seat in the upper half of the lower deck to $63,000 for one of 268 18-seat luxury suites.

• **The Midway Dome**—Very brief consideration was given to doming Midway Stadium in St. Paul.

• **The Coon Rapids Dome**—Just for the record.

• **The Met Dome**—Which included a Met no-dome. Among many options considered at one time or another for the Met stadium complex were plans to (a) dome and enlarge the Met at a cost of up to $40.2 million; (b) build a dome for football on or near the Met for $39 million to $115 million, depending on optional equipment; (c) build an undomed football stadium on or near the Met for $28 million to $90 million, again depending on relative spiffiness.

• **The Eagan Dome**—The most ambitious of the bunch, and the closest of the also-rans, Pete Parranto's $100 million dome, shopping, entertainment and business complex a mile south of I-494 in Eagan would have been floated on industrial revenue bonds, not regular tax levies. In addition, proceeds from the major shopping center it was to include would have been used to help pay off the bonds.

• **The Riverfront Dome**—And last but certainly not least, remember that the original dome proposed for the Industry Square area was along the Mississippi, northeast of the crossing of South Second Street and I-35W. As one Viking official remarked, what better place to tailgate than on the banks of the Father of Waters?

Dick Schaaf is a local free-lance writer whose articles have appeared in numerous national and local publications. He is the co-author of Wheelchair Bowling, *a complete guide to bowling for the handicapped.*

Ralph Rapson's dome in Falcon Heights was one part of World Agromart—a proposed agricultural and convention center development.

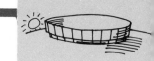

The Portable Dome

Architects:
The Design Collective
Architects, engineers, planners, environmental scientists,
socio-eco-psycho-nutritional analysts, etc.
2929 Fourth Avenue South
Minneapolis   822-4200

The stadium's advantages are numerous:

1. It can be moved anywhere, thus solving the political strife between metropolitan communities.

2. Football fans can watch the first half in Industry Square; during half-time it can be folded up and moved to Bloomington for the second half.

3. Each game, no matter the size of the crowd, can be a "full house" as the stadium need only be inflated to the size of the crowd at hand.

4. It can be moved to another city along with the sport franchise so the city won't be stuck with an empty "white elephant."

5. It won't rust like steel or crack like concrete—just a dab of tire patching here and there will keep it in shape.

6. It saves money on grounds maintenance as it doesn't cover any ground except at game time. The only real expense is updating the truck trailer license tabs.

7. Sports fans can combine their athletic appreciation with their use of CB radios. A fun event would be for the truck driver to motor around giving clues of his whereabouts to CB fans who would try to guess where he's going to set up the stadium.

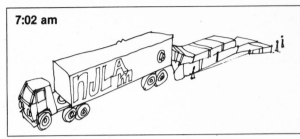

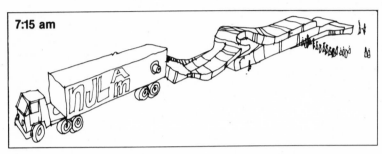

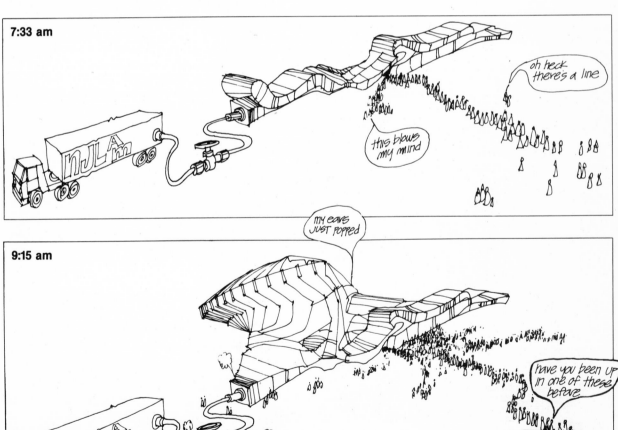

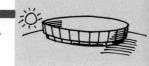

Game Time

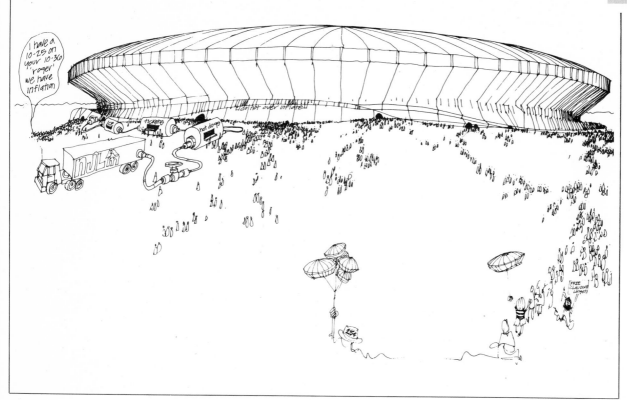

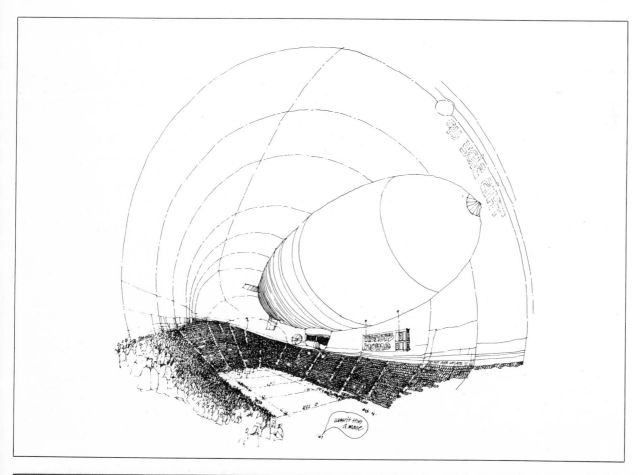

The Making of the Metrodome

by MARC HEQUET

When the Metropolitan Sports Facilities Commission decided in December 1978 that it wanted the downtown Minneapolis site for the domed stadium, it set off a whole new round of warfare between stadium backers and foes. At times during the fight it even appeared that the stadium was beaten. After a hectic day at the Legislature in early 1979, a television reporter told viewers that the stadium was alive—but you needed to hold a mirror to its lips to tell that it was breathing. Nevertheless, the dome showed a staying power that saw it through political and legal skirmishes to completion.

Following the stadium commission's decision on downtown Minneapolis, the Legislature began blasting away in January 1979. It repealed the 2 percent tax on hotels, motels and liquor in the seven-county metropolitan area. Revenues from that tax were to back up stadium bond revenues and pay interest during construction, and repeal seemed to ice the stadium issue. But before the 1979 session ended in May, the Legislature recanted, passing a 3 percent tax limited to Minneapolis. The stadium was back in business.

Then a Minneapolis DFLer, Sen. Jack Davies, swung into action with a petition drive to put the 3 percent tax on the Minneapolis city election ballot in November 1979. The petition drive fell short of the number of signatures needed. Davies went to the City Council, but it said no referendum. He went to Hennepin District Court. It said no referendum. The 3 percent hotel, motel and liquor-by-the-drink tax stood.

The next target was sale of bonds for the stadium, a move that would initiate construction. Minneapolis businessman Bob Short, Senate Majority Leader Nicholas Coleman and Senate Minority Leader Robert Ashbach sued the stadium commission's parent, the Metropolitan Council. The plaintiffs called the bond sale into question because, they said, fees that would be collected by Piper, Jaffray & Hopwood Inc. of Minneapolis, which handled the sale, would be higher than the law allowed. The suit could

A view of the pre-Metrodome downtown Minneapolis skyline as seen from the east.

14

have delayed the bond sale and construction, but stadium backers prevailed—in time for the Oct. 15, 1979, deadline. As it turned out, just four buyers agreed to carry the bond load—three banks and one insurance company, all local—and that meant a relatively small fee for the bond broker.

Meanwhile, there were other hangups. The neighbors were worried. Representatives of Elliot Park and Cedar-Riverside neighborhoods adjacent to the stadium went to the state Environmental Quality Board in 1979 to ask for another environmental impact study before the stadium was built. They feared that the dome would prompt commercial development that could wrack the neighborhoods with traffic and displacement problems. The board said no.

A pair of Minneapolis men sued to stop construction, claiming that the stadium would mean more pollution and that the National Football league and Minnesota Legislature had different television blackout standards for games at the dome. The case was dismissed—a signal to some that the courts were weary of stop-the-dome litigation, and that stadium foes were running out of ammunition.

But that NFL blackout rule looked ominous for a while. Minnesota Vikings brass came back from a winter meeting with the news that NFL owners were sticking by their standard: No local telecast of home games unless all tickets were sold 72 hours before kickoff. The stadium law said only 90 percent of the tickets had to be sold. Legislators worried that, with 15,000 more football seats to fill at the dome, sellouts would be far from certain. Constituents deprived of televised Vikings home games would mean lost votes. But a corporate angel descended to untie the knot. General Mills Inc. pledged up to $1.5 million over 20 years to pay for unsold tickets. In a special look at the dome issue, *Business Week* magazine noted that the dome had time and again forged ahead "with a display of power and tenacity by corporate leaders."

Stadium construction began in December 1979 with excavation of the enormous pit that would hold the dome. Around the pit, 52 concrete columns were driven into the bedrock 50 feet below what would become the playing surface. Atop the columns, the step-like, 110-foot-long concrete slope girders—the stadium "skeleton"—were poured in place.

Over the slope girders went the seating surface and the seats themselves—63,000 for football and 55,000 for baseball, compared with 48,000 football and 41,000 baseball at Metropolitan Stadium in Bloomington. When fans saw the Twins and Vikings play at the Met, they sat in a hodgepodge of armchair and bleacher seats. At the dome, they all sit in blue plastic armchairs. When the occupant rises, the seat springs upright—giving passing beer carriers more elbow room.

Spectators can repair to their choice of 32 restrooms and 39 concession outlets around the stadium. Food and beverage hawkers also circulate, as at the Met. But Minnesota's indoor smoking restrictions apply to indoor stadiums. Nicotine fits require a trip to the concourses or the restrooms for a smoke.

Not that the dome can't ventilate. Its blower system can exchange the stadium's 60 million cubic feet of air in *one hour*. When the sun goes down on a muggy evening, operators hope the dome can suck in enough cool twilight air to lower stadium temperature by several degrees before, say, the fourth inning. For day games, engineers guarantee that the inside temperature won't exceed the reading outdoors. The dome reflects most of the sun's heat, and the stadium taps into the constant 55-degree temperature of the soil surrounding it for additional cooling.

Mark Jensen

A Rock of Ages

On Jan. 2, 1980, during excavation for the Metrodome, an immovable force was encountered by the bulldozers. What first appeared to be just another boulder to be moved, crushed and dispersed turned out to be a 125-ton, 1.8 billion-year-old granite formation that defied most technological attempts to reduce it to an insignificant portion of the 50-yard-line or the base path.

When one considers that the rock supposedly found its way to Minneapolis a mere 11,000 years ago, who can blame it for not wanting to move again? After all, a change of scenery every 11 centuries can be unsettling.

So, the rock resisted all attempts to dislodge it, move it, crush it, blast it. In short, it had the excavators between a rock and . . . well, you get the idea. Meanwhile, it captured local public sentiment and substantial media attention.

By coincidence, First Bank Minneapolis was opening a branch in the western Minneapolis suburb of Plymouth. Bank officials decided that a more natural landmark could not be found for the new branch than . . . "Plymouth Rock."

Nearly two months after it exhibited a will of its own, the rock became a major exhibit as it was loaded onto two side-by-side flatbed trailers, a railroad car, again onto the flatbed trailers and transported to First Bank Minneapolis's Plymouth branch.

And today? The Hubert H. Humphrey Metrodome is complete. Players play. Cheerleaders cheer. Crowds applaud. And the rock breathes a sigh of relief that it may not have to move for another 10,998 years.

In cold weather, the building is heated. From season to season, its temperature should range between 60 and 90 degrees.

For another measure of what the dome's air-handling system can do, consider that it supports a roof that, with fixtures, weighs 340 tons. The entire NFL Players Association only weighs about 140 tons. Twenty 90-horsepower fans hold up fabric, steel cables, public address fixtures and lights. If the dome ever came down again as it did in November 1981, roof, cables and fixtures would settle suspended well above seats and playing field, say designers.

The woven fiberglass roof is in two layers, with the outer layer's exterior surface coated with Teflon for weatherproofing. Each layer is 1/32 inch thick and is clamped to steel cables up to 750 feet long that crisscross the stadium. The inner and outer layers are separated by as much as six feet, and between them warm air circulates to melt snow and ice. The November 1981 collapse was a victory of weather over planning. There was too much snow and, at that stage of construction, too little heat.

Stadium builders installed the roof a section at a time beginning in June 1981. The dome was inflated in October 1981, when playful workers bounded across the roof like moonwalkers. Between them and the construction jumble on the stadium floor below were 187 feet—of air.

A little exuberance was permissible. Moving 600,000 cubic yards of dirt and putting up 40,000 cubic yards of concrete and 500 tons of steel is a lot of work. At times as many as 600 workers from the stadium's 80 contractors were on the site. Like any big construction job, the dome had its labor disputes. Ironworkers and bricklayers haggled over who would drive bolts into the concrete, prompting a two-day walkout by about 30 workers. A bigger work stoppage was threatened when union workers charged that a contractor was using nonunion labor. But that was settled and the workers stayed on. The unions had agreed to a no-strike contract—and that saved the stadium commission from hundreds of thousands of dollars in lost work time when other Minneapolis construction workers struck in early 1981. At the stadium, work went on.

There were other construction glitches too—many magnified in the public eye by reporters scrutinizing what they saw as a major statewide story from the word go. When inspectors discovered five weakened slant girders, the media picked up the story. Stadium commission executive director Don Poss called the improperly reinforced structures a routine construction slip, not hard to fix. Such a matter at another construction site wouldn't make headlines, Poss said. (The stadium commission hired an independent engineer, who brought the girders up to standard.)

The stadium wound up within the $55 million construction limit set by the Legislature. As construction went on, contractors scrambled for business, lowering their bids and holding down the overall cost. Other cost-savers: The stadium commission acted as its own general contractor, hiring subcontractors for the work. And fast-track, plan-as-you-go construction permitted work to begin eight or nine months earlier than if plans had all been worked out ahead of time. Inflation during those months would have fattened the cost of the stadium significantly.

But the dome was always more than a money issue. It raised the question of how much government should be involved in private-sector sports, and that set ablaze two Minnesota passions: politics and team loyalty to the Twins and Vikings. Indeed, stadium commissioner Ron Gornick, who was the swing vote on the 4-3 decision to build in downtown Minneapolis, told the Minneapolis *Star* he cast a downtown dome vote because he feared the Vikings would leave town if they didn't get a dome.

The decision split the state down the middle and landed the stadium commission in court again and again. All told, it spent $750,000 on legal fees getting the downtown dome erected. Despite the expense, the commission preferred legal opposition to the illegal kind. Executive Director Poss said privately in 1978 that the windows of his car had been shot out at his suburban home, the Minneapolis *Star* reported. Following the decision to build in downtown Minneapolis, a man who said he had a gun made threatening remarks at the commission's St. Paul office. Later, the office was evacuated because of a bomb threat.

There have been bigger, more complex building projects, but few fought over as lustily. Even with work about to begin, the stadium looked like anything but a sure bet. But there it stands.

The Day the Dome Went Down

Just 48 days after an elaborate ceremony marking the inflation of the Metrodome, the first heavy snow of the winter season arrived and the dome went down.

The stadium's roof, after partially collapsing the day before, completely deflated under the weight of 10.2 inches of heavy, wet snow. Stadium authorities blamed the deflation on a large rip in the roof, caused by a puncture in a panel of the fabric on the north side of the stadium. There were no injuries, and the roof was repaired and reinflated four days later, before the next snow could have done more serious damage.

The rip was caused when a bolt snapped, bending a piece of steel which slashed through the fabric roof. The roof is kept in place by air pressure from up to 20 fans inside the stadium, and the dome collapsed when air escaped through the hole.

News of the deflation, along with the heaviest Twin Cities snowfall since Nov. 17, 1978, was carried on all three network evening news shows and was featured at halftime and before games the following Sunday and Monday on various National Football League telecasts.

Marc Hequet is a freelance writer living in St. Paul.

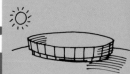

Only 28 months passed between the breaking of ground for the Metrodome and the first scheduled event, an exhibition baseball game between the Minnesota Twins and the Philadelphia Phillies on April 3, 1982. The biggest physical obstacle encountered was the 125-ton Plymouth Rock (below).

Metrodome construction commenced in December 1979 with massive "ground breaking" excavations that saw 600,000 cubic yards of dirt removed from the site. Then, circling the pit, 52 concrete columns were pounded into the bedrock 50 feet below playing field level. The stadium climbed into the skyline when the columns were topped with a concrete-girder skeleton. As many as 600 workers were on site during peak building periods. They poured 40,000 cubic yards of concrete, hefted 500 tons of structural steel into place and stretched the 340-ton fiberglass roof over the 9.5-acre area—all within budget and on schedule.

The Comforts of Home in Private Boxes

There are 115 private boxes on the top of the lower concourse at the Humphrey Metrodome. Forty-six private suites contain eight seats, 56 have 10 seats, and 13 have 12 seats. The front facing window of each suite is approximately 50 feet above the playing field and 150 feet from the football sidelines.

The annual base charge for seats is $25,000 per box for the 8-seat boxes; $27,500 per suite for the 10-seat boxes, and $30,000 per year for the 12-seat suites. Each suite has two levels, a lower level facing the playing field with armchair seating, and an upper level with color-coordinated furniture and seating. Suites also include built-in cabinetry, a wardrobe, sink, under-counter refrigerator, ice maker and color television. Suites are equipped with electrical outlets and telephones.

Admission tickets to Viking games are included with the suites, and suite holders may purchase up to 10 additional season tickets immediately in front of the suite. For all other events, the suite holders have the right to purchase admission tickets in the number up to the seating capacity of the private box. Most of the private boxes are held by Twin Cities corporations.

Nicollet Park: Home of the Millers

by DAVE MONA

A classy page was torn out of baseball history when Nicollet Park's right-field fence—only 279 feet down the line—was ripped down.

It was 25 years ago that a functional concrete, glass and brick bank went up where the soggy, foul, rotten and thoroughly wonderful Nicollet Park once stood on the one-half city block bounded by W. 31st St. between Nicollet and Blaisdell Avs.

In 1955, the year before its razing, Nicollet Park saw the old Minneapolis Millers win their first and only Little World Series in the final game played in the cozy matchbox.

Newspapers the next morning ran a large picture of the old wooden park, filled beyond capacity, under the words:

"Nicollet's Last and Greatest Hour."

But, in bars from Lake Street to Lake City and amusement rooms from Ada to Zumbrota, people old enough to remember and sentimental enough to care still talk about Joe Hauser's record 69 home runs, Mike Kelley's right fielder-terrorizing dogs and that marvelous month of May 1951 when a kid named Mays came to town.

People may profess to like Calvin Griffith's Twins, but there's little arguing that people loved the Minneapolis Millers.

Dave Moore, WCCO TV's newscaster since pre-Twins days, recalls going over to Nicollet Park from KUOM Radio's studios on the University of Minnesota campus.

In the group of 1950s broadcasters was one Ray Christensen, now WCCO Radio's play-by-play man on University of Minnesota football and basketball.

"We used to sit out in the left field bleachers and then Christensen would start in with his play-by-play," Moore recalled. "We'd all groan and ask, 'Do you want to sit by him?'

"There might be only 500 people in the park and you could hear Ray all over. It was really embarrassing. I can close my eyes and still hear him saying, 'Jack Cassini at the plate. Big number three on the back of his gray St. Paul Saints road uniform.'"

Christensen doesn't dispute Moore's recollections. In fact, he sounds rather proud of them.

"There was a wonderful intimacy about that place," he said. "There really wasn't a bad seat. You could hear conversations among the players and even see their faces.

"And another thing you don't see anymore is that everybody knew all the batting averages and numbers of all the players. And you hated the opposition. Every opposing player was the enemy."

Nicollet, the Millers and the American Association had a certain kind of class.

Any league that could boast the Toledo Mud Hens for 50 years had to have class.

Even the worst seats at Nicollet Park were close to the playing field.

From 1915 until 1952 the league operated with the same eight teams. Railroads linked the eastern division teams from Louisville, Indianapolis, Toledo and Columbus and the western cities of Milwaukee, Kansas City, Minneapolis and St. Paul. Within 10 years of the demise of the original eight, the western division cities all received major league franchises.

Nicollet Park was built in 1896, six years before the American Association was formed.

Not long after the start of Association play, in a park known for thousands of "cheap" home runs, came baseball's shortest.

Fleet Andy Oyler, the Miller shortstop, was batting in the late innings of a game played in a steady drizzle. Those were days when it was unusual to use a half dozen baseballs per game.

The pitch was low and Oyler chopped it, sending it straight down into the mud in front of home plate. As Oyler circled the bases, the pitcher and catcher appealed for help and the entire infield began to dig for the darkened baseball.

Oyler slid across home plate just seconds in front of a futile tag by the second baseman who had unearthed the ball 5½ feet from home plate, establishing a home run record that is certainly more secure than even Hank Aaron's.

It was in its salad years that the park saw one of its biggest and best brawls. Both teams were about to converge upon umpire Brick Owens when Pudge Heffelfinger, Yale's three-time All America football guard from Minnesota, jumped onto the field and saved Owens by offering to take on combatants from both teams.

The Millers were perhaps as well known for their rhubarbs as their home runs.

The late sportswriter and sportscaster Halsey Hall, who allegedly sat at Abner Doubleday's right hand when the latter invented baseball, once recalled that the Millers' most memorable riot occurred in St. Paul at old Lexington Park on July 4, 1929.

"The St. Paul pitcher covered first on a bunt and was spiked by our runner [Hall identified with the Millers in cross-city games]. The pitcher threw the ball at the runner, and the Millers' first-base coach decked the pitcher. Both benches emptied and it took 20 minutes to clear the field," Hall said.

"It was one of those holiday split double-headers [morning game in one city, afternoon game in the other] and there was a full house at Nicollet in the afternoon. But, like so many of those affairs, the afternoon game was peaceful."

In 1954, the Millers, under manager Bill Rigney, took part in one of baseball's largest enforced exoduses. Jim Constable was pitching for Minneapolis, Herb Score for

CONCESSION PRICES

PLEASE NOTE: All Vendors have Uniform numbers. Any complaint can only be rectified when having exact Uniform numbers.

Red Hots	20c	Grain Belt Beer	30c
Popcorn	15c	Gluek's Beer	30c
Salted in Shell		Coffee	10c
Peanuts	10c	Cushions	10c
Candy	10c	Cigarettes	25c
Coca-Cola	15c	Cigarettes (King size)	30c
Orange	15c	Cigars	10c
Potato Chips	10c	Sporting News	25c
Hot Chocolate	15c	Miniature	
Crest Ice Cream	15c	Bats	35c and 50c

In 1955 you could get a hot dog, popcorn, peanuts, pop, potato chips, ice cream and a program for less than a dollar.

Indianapolis and Stan Landes was umpiring. Early in the game, Score, the Association's all-time strikeout leader, hit a Miller batter with a fast ball. Three innings later, Constable hit Score with a slow curve. Landes, never a popular local figure, threw Constable out of the game for deliberately hitting Score.

Rigney charged onto the field and explained to Landes, loud enough to be heard without any amplification in the Twin Cities Rapid Transit stables across 31st Street, that if Constable were planning to hit Score, he wouldn't have done it with a slow curve.

Landes told Rigney that he didn't need a lecture on the finer points of beanballing, and he ordered Rigney from the field. At that point the Miller dugout jockeys took after Landes, and two more players were invited to leave.

"Why don't you throw them all out?" chided Rigney, who was waiting around to see how it was all going to end.

"That's not a bad idea," replied Landes, and to the showers went the entire Miller team except for Chico Ibanez, a Spanish-speaking utility infielder who was taking a siesta in the right field bullpen.

The Mike Kelley era is probably the most talked about in Miller history. From 1928 through 1937 the Irishman made money and friends by doing a thriving business in retooling old ballplayers.

"He used to build his team around that right field fence," recalled George Brophy, Millers business manager and now director of minor league operations for the Minnesota Twins.

"He'd take a strong left-handed hitter and give him a full year of play where he'd hit 30 home runs and never have to chase a ball in right field. Then he'd sell him to the big leagues for a bundle of cash and some more players.

"He used to break even on expenses and gate receipts and make his profit selling players. Most of the guys he sold to the majors never did anything again after they left Minneapolis and that right field fence."

Brophy told of Nicollet's biggest crowd: "One day Mike got stiff and told the ushers not to close the gates. There were 15,216 people there that day in a park built for 8,500, if you could get the people to sit close enough together in the bleachers.

"They were sitting along the foul lines and when the umpires demanded that the fans get off the field, Mike invited some to sit in the dugout."

Hall used to tell the tale of Kelley's big Dalmatians who used to wander onto the field and growl at opposing right fielders. One day, Hall said, a Milwaukee right fielder refused to chase a long fly because he was paralyzed with fright by the dogs.

Part of Nicollet's lore exists in the realm of hard to believe (and hard to verify) anecdotes . . . those kind of stories your uncle's barber's neighbor allegedly witnessed.

Some fans say they were there the day an anonymous Miller stole first. The story has it that the player bunted his way to first and stole second on the first pitch to the next batter. Then, on the next pitch, he raced back to first while the befuddled catcher just held onto the ball and stared. Not even Halsey Hall, who for many years broadcast both Millers and Twins games, could confirm that one.

Dave Moore's favorite eyewitness account took place in the mid-'30s when Bill Norman, Saints' left fielder, came in for a high fly ball, looked up, stopped in his tracks, turned green and passed out. He had swallowed his cud of chewing tobacco.

It was at Nicollet that Ab Wright hit four home runs and a triple in five at bats and was on deck when the game ended. The 19 total bases is a record that still stands.

It was also at Nicollet that a young outfielder named Ted Williams won the league batting title in 1938 with a .366 average and showed that he possessed an equally fearsome temper.

According to stories, he once dropped a fly ball, picked it up, dropped it again, picked it up, dropped it, picked it

The 1955 Millers were Little World Series Champions and the last team to play in Nicollet Park. Top Row: Al Corwin, Al Olson, Joe Margoneri, Jim Constable, Alex Konikowski, Carl Sawatski, Ron Northey; Middle Row: Art Ruane, Monte Irvin, Don Bollweg, Floyd Melliere, Bud Byerly, Harry Nicholas, Fred Richards, Al Worthington, Tom McKenna; Front Row: Lou Ortiz, Ray Dabek, Rance Pless, Ray Mueller, Bill Rigney, Bob Lennon, Joe Brachitta, George Wilson; Bat Boy: John Mueller; Inset: Red Mottlow, Millers Baseball Broadcaster, WLOL.

TICKET INFORMATION

— PRICES —

	Box	Reserved	Grandstand	Bleachers
Adults	$1.75	$1.40	$1.10	$0.70
Children under 12	1.15	.80	.50	.35
Ladies on Ladies' Night Only (Tuesdays)	1.00	.65	.35	.35

Nicollet Park Office

3048 Nicollet Avenue

RE. 3900

Ladies' Night Every Tuesday

Downtown Ticket Office

BILLY & MARTY'S CIGAR STORE

609 Marquette — FI. 2462

**Telephone Reservations must be picked up the day before the game is to be played.
No orders can be accepted on the day of the game.**

Miller tickets in the 1950s ranged from 35 cents to $1.75. Another way to get in was to catch a foul ball or home run during batting practice and exchange the ball for a ticket.

up for a final time and threw it over the fence.

In 1951, the New York Giants, with whom the Millers had a working agreement, assigned Willie Mays to Minneapolis. In 35 games he collected 71 hits, 8 home runs and 30 runs batted in. He was batting a torrid .477 when the call came from manager Leo Durocher in New York.

Giants owner Horace Stoneham bought space in the newspapers to explain that Mays was necessary to the Giants' title hopes and that he was sorry for the plight of the Millers. The Giants, with Mays, won the title on Bobby Thomson's home run against the Dodgers. The Millers, without Mays, barely finished in the first division.

In the Little World Series of 1955, the Miller pitching hero was big Allan Worthington, who won three games and saved the final and last game for the Millers in a harbinger of the relief role he was to play with the Twins a decade later. Worthington's crucial save came in the last game ever played at Nicollet.

The Millers set a league record with 241 homers that year. Ten different players hit 12 or more home runs. The team batting average was .281 with seven players over .300.

To the players, Nicollet meant inadequate dressing facilities to be shared equally with the rats and termites. There were holes in the dressing room walls, and the floor was buckled where the foundation had shifted over the years.

To the fans, Nicollet meant slivers from the wooden seats, gloves left on the field when players hit, autographs and knothole days when 10 cents or a returned foul ball was good for one bleacher seat. It also meant ushers who offered you tickets in exchange for foul balls and who hinted strongly that you'd be wise to go for the tickets.

To the news media, mostly newspapermen in those days, it meant the wonderful press box built for the 1939 All-Star game. The facilities were cozy, but it was suggested that you stand and lean forward if you wanted to see all of the field.

To the management, it meant trouble with fire and police officials about inadequate exits into Nicollet Avenue traffic. It meant a constant duel with owners of Nicollet Avenue businesses about broken windows caused by pop-fly home runs over right field's 40-foot-high fence and screen.

"We had so many windows broken in the President Cafe and Johnson's Appliances that only Lloyd's of London would insure us by the time we moved out," Brophy said.

"I remember that we were never too worried about a fire because the wood was so rotten that it wouldn't burn."

There was no on-site parking, and home owners in the area constantly complained about cars parked in front of their homes.

Opposing managers used to stall until 6 p.m. on Sundays because of a city ordinance against any inning starting after that time. Pop bottles and rented cushions used to greet any opposing manager who dared to change pitchers at 5:45 p.m. in the fourth inning.

Years later someone checked and no such ordinance was found.

Two years before the park was demolished, someone checked the distance to first base and found that it was 88 feet instead of the standard 90. It wasn't chicanery, an official explained; the park had merely shrunk with age.

This feature has been edited from a story Dave Mona wrote in 1966 as a reporter for the Minneapolis Tribune.

Lexington Park: Campy, The Duke, The Babe, and Oh, That Coliseum!

by PATRICK REUSSE

Marty O'Neill, the play-by-play announcer for the St. Paul Saints, was visiting the Brooklyn Dodgers' spring training complex at Vero Beach, Fla., and one of the first people to recognize Marty was the catcher, Roy Campanella.

The previous summer, in 1948, Campanella had been assigned by the Dodgers to St. Paul. Along with playing a spectacular brand of baseball, Campanella was in St. Paul to help break the color barrier in the American Association. It was an eventful stay. The Campanellas' first child was born in St. Paul. And, in 35 games, Campanella batted .325. More notably, he hit 13 home runs in a mere 123 at-bats.

Campanella approached O'Neill that next spring and said, "Marty, I liked that city of yours. I'd like to go back to St. Paul some day. Nice city, nice people."

"And then Campy gave me the biggest smile in the world," O'Neill recalled, "and he said, 'And oh, that Coliseum!'"

The Coliseum was the landmark of Lexington Park, the home of baseball in St. Paul from 1897 until 1956. The history of the St. Paul Saints is the history of Lexington Park, and the roof of the Coliseum became a part of that history in 1916.

It was the Coliseum Pavilion, a dance hall that shared the left-field wall with the ball park, and it was paradise for righthanded power hitters such as Campanella.

It was 315 feet down the left field line at Lexington, and it was possible to wrap a line drive around the foul pole and miss the Coliseum. But most of the home runs in Lexington floated over the convenient power alley in left center and nestled on the Coliseum roof. "Campanella hit a few beyond the Coliseum roof," O'Neill said. "If Campy would have played a whole season in Lexington, only God knows how many he would have hit."

As delightful a playground as Lexington was for Campanella and his righthanded compadres, it was difficult for lefthanded hitters (and right fielders).

The right-field fence rose on a bank to the foul pole, which was 361 feet from home plate. From there, it went out sharply, to straightaway center field, 472 feet. It made Yankee Stadium's infamous Death Valley look like a chip shot. "You could spend a summer at Lexington and not see more than a dozen home runs hit to right center," O'Neill said. "Duke Snider could handle the distance, and the oldtimers liked to talk about the visit Babe Ruth made here in 1928."

Snider, like Campanella a Hall of Famer, played in St. Paul for 66 games in 1946. Tom Mee, later the public relations director for the Saints and now for the Minnesota Twins, was in the service then. He recalled the letters from home being filled with information about Snider.

"Duke was a 19-year-old then, and apparently everyone in town was going to the ball park to see this kid hit one over the scoreboard," Mee said. "It had to be 400 feet to the base of the scoreboard in right center, and Duke cleared it a couple of times."

Campy. The Duke. And the Babe.

Ruth was in Lexington for an exhibition game in 1928, when the Saints were a farm club of the Yankees. Ruth visited the St. Paul newspaper offices in downtown. He autographed baseballs and then tossed them to a mob of fans that were waiting in the street below.

Then, the Babe went to Lexington and hit a couple of home runs over that scoreboard in right, although reports conflict now. Some stories say he hit it over the scoreboard in batting practice, others say it was in the game. The only certainty is that the Babe took some swings at Lexington. He probably ran up the bank in right to shag fly balls, too.

You still can see that incline in the parking lot of the shopping complex that sits where Lexington used to be—between Lexington and Dunlap, just off University Avenue.

That was the site on which, on April 30, 1897, a fellow named Charles Comiskey built a ball park for his St. Paul Saints. It was the first of two Lexington Parks, and it was billed as a park with "no superiors, including such unheard of innovations as backs on bleacher seats and the finest English grass available in the outfield."

The Saints opened their new ball park that day with a 10-3 victory over Milwaukee, a team that was under the direction of a chap named Connie Mack.

Five years later, the American Association was formed, with St. Paul as a member. In 1916, the park was rebuilt and home plate was moved from the Lexington to the Dunlap side of the acreage.

That left room for the new dance hall in left. Above the right field fence, and beyond a second fence at the top of a bank, was a company called Keys Well Drilling. Mr. Keys constructed a large sign on top of his building so people who came to the ball park and might some day need a well drilled knew where to call.

It was in that ball park the St. Paul Saints played for 40 years, skipping only 1918 when the season was cancelled by World War I. There was a crisis in the mid-'30s, when owner Bob Connery threatened to move the franchise to,

get this, Peoria, but Connery was bought out by local interests. Lights were installed in 1937 and there was a pennant in 1938.

That was followed by a lengthy decline under a working agreement with the White Sox, Comiskey's team. It took from opening day of 1939 until June of 1943 for the Saints to rise as high as fifth place in the American Association. There was another war to worry about then, and attendance fell dramatically, all the way to 74,000 in 1942.

Then, the war was over and the Dodgers were the new partners. On opening day of 1946, a record crowd of 21,000 jammed into a stadium built for 17,000. Fans circled the outfield a dozen deep. By the end of the season, the Duke and his teammates had attracted 290,000.

The Dodgers bought the Saints outright in 1947 and attendance hit a record 353,010 in 1949. No one talked about Lexington being antiquated. But, by the mid-'50s, major league fever had hit the Twin Cities and St. Paul

For more than half a century St. Paul fans watched their team from the cozy confines of Lexington Park.

decided to get into the sweepstakes with a new ball park.

The final baseball game was played in Lexington on Sept. 5, 1956, when 19-year-old Stan Williams beat—most appropriately—the Minneapolis Millers, by 4-0. The attendance was 2,227 and the season total was 102,004, the lowest since World War II. Lexington was demolished by early 1957.

A fan in that last-night crowd mourned the passing of Lexington. "They should play here forever," he said. "In the old days, the fans would circle the outfield and, if the ball went into the crowd, it was a double. When St. Paul came to bat, the crowd would move closer toward home plate, and then the fans would retreat when Minneapolis batted. Those were the days."

Twenty-five years later, Marty O'Neill agrees.

"I drive by that shopping center once in awhile," O'Neill said. "I get thinking about what used to be there, and the times we had, and I have a tendency to get tears in my eyes."

Oh, that Coliseum.

It was an easy streetcar ride from a morning game at St. Paul's Lexington Park, pictured here, to the afternoon game at Minneapolis' Nicollet Park. For years, the teams played split double headers on the 4th of July.

Patrick Reusse is a sports columnist for the St. Paul Dispatch *and Sunday* Pioneer Press.

Memorial Stadium: As Many Memories as There are Bricks

by CHUCK BENDA

The fans were eager to see their football team play in a modern stadium. Nearly 500 of them gathered in a March snowstorm in Minneapolis to watch the ground-breaking ceremony for the new stadium. They were excited about the large seating capacity of the new stadium. It was very frustrating when you couldn't get tickets for the big games. Other football teams around the league had built, or were planning to build, new stadiums—stadiums that held 60,000, or even 80,000 fans. Why not Minnesota?

The whole city watched as the construction went on at a rapid pace. Four hundred seventy-five construction workers were working on the stadium and gradually the bowl-shaped walls began to rise, taking a prominent place on the Minneapolis skyline. In fact, it was nearly impossible to ignore the massive structure as it neared completion. The stadium was finished ahead of schedule and well within its allotted budget—*$650,000!*

No, not $65 million, $650,000. The year was 1924 and the stadium was the University of Minnesota's Memorial Stadium. Howard Cosell hadn't learned his first ten-dollar word yet and Monday Night Football was the extra-long practice sessions the Gophers put in after they lost to an underdog, but thousands of fans were willing to line up and pay as much as $2.50 apiece for a seat in the new stadium. (Ticket prices varied with the reputation of the opponent. A ticket to a game with the lowly Flickertails of North Dakota was only $1. Michigan or Illinois could command $2.50.)

Built in 1924 as a replacement for Northrop Field, which had a seating capacity of 20,000, Memorial Stadium, or the Brick House, as it came to be known, was hailed by some as the eighth wonder of the world. The following excerpt from the October 9, 1924 edition of the *Minnesota Alumni Weekly* demonstrated the enthusiasm for it:

"Drawing like a great horseshoe magnet, Minnesota's great Memorial Stadium drew . . . the largest crowd that ever saw an opening football game at the University of Minnesota . . . . Makers of Minnesota football history . . . were . . . shouting their approval of the stadium with its 1,000,000 bricks, its 18 miles of redwood seats, and its 10,500 cubic yards of concrete."

For 57 years the Brick House was the Saturday afternoon home of thousands of football fans each autumn. From the lean early years, through the "Age of Bierman" when the Gophers became "Golden" by winning six conference championships and four national championships in eight years under Coach Bernie Bierman, and on to the trying decades that followed—the Gophers have not won a conference championship outright in 40 years—Gopher fans have showed up in the Brick House to keep the tradition alive.

Even through the losing seasons in 100 years of football at Minnesota, although attendance may have fallen off, there was always a solid core of fan support for the Gophers. When the idea of building a new stadium was brought up in 1921, the Gophers had just completed one of their worst seasons, winning only one game and losing seven. Yet they were still able to fill Northrop Field to

A number of Paul Giel's football records at Minnesota lasted for more than 25 years.

overflowing, and when the call went out for pledges of financial support to build a new stadium, the needed money was raised in the first week of the 1922 fundraising campaign.

Construction began on March 6, 1924. The new stadium was to be a memorial to Minnesotans who died in World War I. By October 4, just six months later, the stadium was completed and ready for the opening game of the 1924 season. The Gophers beat the Flickertails of North Dakota 14-0 as 16,000 fans watched. The victory over

North Dakota was only a moderate success since the Gophers were expected to beat them by at least 30 points, but the stadium was a big hit.

Pictures of the new stadium were published in almost every local paper and University publication. Fred Luehring, athletic director at the time, wrote a story for a University paper extolling the virtues of the stadium. An architecture professor demonstrated how the stadium was specially designed to meet the particular needs of the University of Minnesota.

With the growing enthusiasm came larger crowds. Although the capacity of the stadium is variously listed as being from 51,000 to 57,000, the second Michigan game of 1926 drew 60,000 fans. (At times, chairs have been set on the running track that circles the field, and the seating capacity of the bleachers added at the west end of the stadium has varied through the years. The largest crowd

on record at Memorial Stadium was 66,284 at the Nov. 18, 1961 Purdue game.)

The fans continued to fill the stadium in the following years and the ticket revenue filled the coffers of the athletic department. These monies were used to build, either wholly or in part, the Field House, Williams Arena, Bierman Field, and the University Golf Course.

Unfortunately, Memorial Stadium was never quite as marvelous as it was cracked up to be. A flaw in the design of the stadium had the rows of benches rising along a curved line like the inside of a bowl rather than in a straight line. This provides poor sightlines to the playing field for thousands of fans who must constantly stretch their necks to see over the fans in front of them. The bench-like plank seats are without backrests and often become quite uncomfortable after a half of football.

The seats in the east end of the U-shaped stadium became very unpopular because they were so far from the playing field. The field was shifted to improve those seats, but this left the press boxes too far toward the other end of the field. The press boxes came to be known as perhaps the worst in any major college stadium.

The end of Memorial Stadium actually began to come about in 1958. At that time, University President J.L. Morrill appointed an advisory committee to examine the stadium and suggest solutions. No major renovations had been undertaken since construction, and the natural deterioration that came with the passing of time increased the need for

Memorial Stadium held up to 65,000 fans before fire marshals cracked down in the mid 1960s.

Football's Little Brown Jug returned surprisingly to Minnesota after the Gophers' shutout of top-ranked Michigan in 1977.

some sort of action. The advisory committee recommended that nothing be done to Memorial Stadium. It suggested that the University acquire a site for a new stadium, since remodeling wasn't considered feasible.

There was no money in 1958 for new football stadiums. From 1958 until 1972, the University had neither undertaken any major renovations of the Brick House nor acquired a site for a new stadium. The additional years furthered the deterioration. In 1972, when the push was on for a new, multi-use stadium for the Twin Cities, the University looked at the feasibility of remodeling and doming Memorial Stadium. In 1975 and again in 1979, certain factions of the state legislature began to push for a remodeled Memorial Stadium as the solution to the Twin Cities' need for a new stadium. But the plan never received much favor. In fact, in 1975, the Minnesota Vikings said they were not interested in playing in a remodeled stadium, anywhere.

When at last the Industry Square site was settled on for the location of the Hubert H. Humphrey Metrodome, it seemed inevitable that the Brick House would have to go. Without $10 million to $15 million in repairs before 1990, Memorial Stadium would violate the Minneapolis building codes. With the new domed stadium less than two miles away from the Brick House—within walking distance of the West Bank of the Minneapolis campus—and with heavy demands on University funds, playing in the Metrodome

became the best solution to the Memorial Stadium problem.

There was, and is, some resistance among fans who hate to see Gopher football move off campus, but there is also considerable support for the move. Many fans hope, along with the Gopher coaching staff, that the move will help revitalize the football program and, indirectly, the entire athletic program at the University. Many others are happy about the improved seating and the protection from the harsh Minnesota weather in late November.

It will be several years before Memorial Stadium is demolished, since it houses handball courts, weight training rooms, locker rooms, and many offices that cannot be immediately replaced, but an empty football stadium is an inefficient way to use valuable land on a crowded campus. The Brick House will fall. When it does, perhaps there will be a lineup—as there was when the University sold souvenir strips of the Tartan Turf that was removed from the stadium in 1977—to buy souvenir bricks. There are a million of those bricks, but if all the fans that have watched a Gopher game in the Brick House come back, there won't be enough to go around. Save me a brick.

Chuck Benda is Associate Editor of Minnesota Magazine, *the official publication of the University of Minnesota Alumni Association.*

Midway Stadium: Built to Lure the Big Leagues

by PATRICK REUSSE

It was supposed to put St. Paul in the big leagues. Now, at least for a time, it has been turned over to the seagulls.

A couple of large mounds of dirt rest in the middle of the huge, empty field of gravel and clay. There are small pools of standing water, and the gulls sit nearby, resting in the sun.

There is not much action on the railroad tracks that overlook the place from a nearby bank. On the horizon to the north you can see the Minnesota State Fair's Space Needle. It's after Labor Day and it's quiet there now, too.

An energy park, a $250 million project, is scheduled to be constructed here. "It is, indeed, a proposal to capture the imagination of one and all," said an editorialist from St. Paul.

Funny. That's about what the folks in St. Paul were saying about Midway Stadium when construction began on this site 25 years earlier.

The only evidence that remains of Midway Stadium—of St. Paul's big league aspirations—is a sign on Snelling Avenue that reads, "Rosen Road, Midway Stadium," with an arrow pointing you toward the empty field. That sign will be changed soon.

Midway Stadium was dismantled in April of 1981, the site sold to the planners of the energy park for $2.8 million. When major league baseball came to Met Stadium in Bloomington, Midway found its place in Twin Cities folklore as the first of St. Paul's "White Elephants."

Calvin Griffith announced after the 1960 season he was moving the Washington Senators to the Twin Cities. He would call the team the Minnesota Twins, in recognition of the bond between Minneapolis and St. Paul.

That was uncommonly solid PR on Calvin's part, but as far as St. Paulites were concerned, the move to Bloomington meant Minneapolis. It meant St. Paul had lost another battle, maybe its most important in the long-standing, oft-silent war between the neighbors on each side of the river.

Midway Stadium opened on April 25, 1957, with a day-night doubleheader (Calvin made that separate-admission twinbill one of his trademarks later in our baseball history) between the St. Paul Saints and Wichita Braves. The home team lost both games—7-2 before 10,169 fans in the afternoon, 9-1 before 5,850 at night.

For the first game, Mayor Joseph Dillon tossed the first ball to a catcher named Orville Freeman, Minnesota's governor. But it was not for this occasion Midway was built. All of the conversation was of how easily Midway could be expanded to the 35,000 to 40,000 seats that would be required by a major league team, about what a superior facility it was to its counterpart in Bloomington.

"We felt we had a better ballpark," Tom Mee said. "Wider aisles, better sightlines, a better location, with the fairgrounds right next door. The major league talk was at its peak back then, '57 and '58, and St. Paul thought it had a chance. By 1960, everyone was getting cynical. . . . There was a feeling neither city was going to get a team."

Mee was then the public relations director for the Saints. On Oct. 26, 1960, he was driving toward Midway when he heard on the radio that Griffith was moving the Senators to Bloomington. It would be improper to say Mee shot past Midway and headed for the Met, but he did wind up working for the Twins, and has been their PR director since 1962.

The American Association received $600,000 for giving up territorial rights for the St. Paul franchise. St. Paul? It was left with its white elephant, but don't tell that to Ed Delaney Jr.

Delaney's father, Ed Sr., was the mayor of St. Paul when the bond issue that included a new municipal stadium was passed. With his father and most of the other planners now dead, it was Ed Jr. who tried to fight city hall and kill the plan to demolish Midway.

What others saw as a drain on taxpayers Delaney saw as an excellent, multi-purpose, recreational asset, a facility that came so close to paying for itself that it was a violation of the public trust not to retain it.

Delaney started a Save Midway Stadium group and enlisted in his camp city athletic directors and coaches, officials from the nearby colleges of Hamline and Macalester, coaches of amateur and American Legion baseball teams, and many others.

"The city owed $770,000 on 2½ percent bonds on Midway," Delaney said. "We had estimates that it would take $8 million to $9 million to duplicate that stadium today, and companies were willing to insure Midway for $5 million to $6 million. Yet, City Hall sold it for $2.8 million."

Delaney was able to get his point across to the people involved in amateur sports, people who had come to appreciate Midway as a convenient place to hold their events. But he never could stir indignation among the masses. That white-elephant image had been shoved at St. Paulites for so long that it can be assumed many people merely wanted the place to go, to vanish.

It did, with little in the way of a sendoff. Only the gulls are left to appreciate Midway.

The most prominent big leaguers to tread on Midway

were the Vikings, who used it as their September practice facility for years. They abandoned Midway, too, moving to the swank digs in Eden Prairie in the fall of 1981.

Try as we might, we cannot forget here the Minnesota Norsemen and their forebears, the Goofys. They played professional slowpitch softball at Midway for three summers. You missed that, too, huh?

And there were the Twin Cities Lakers, a semi-pro football team that held tryouts at Midway, and practiced there. Alas, the Lakers went belly-up before they played their first game.

There were concerts that packed the place and there were wrestling wars that did the same . . . battle royals and death matches. It was at Midway that Del Flanagan, St. Paul's boxing contender of the '50s, thrashed Gil Turner.

But mostly, Midway had become a place for the amateurs. Many of the 10,250 seats had fallen into disrepair, in need of a fresh coat of paint at the very least.

The Vikings did their best to destroy the turf each September, rooting about as football players must. The repair work needed after they left each fall made them, according to Delaney, an unnecessary client.

"Midway had been operating in the black in recent years . . . about $50,000 per," Delaney said. "It was a great place for the amateurs, and—with a concert or two—they were paying for the place."

But not for the retirement of those low-interest bonds. The folks from city hall took the $2.8 million to pay off the bonds, and to dream of the tax revenues that might be available in the future from the energy park.

And, as a fellow from St. Paul wrote when he visited the empty lot shortly after the stadium was dismantled, this way people would not have Midway to kick around anymore.

There are big plans for the Midway site now. But there were big plans back when the ball park was new and shiny. Check out this, from the St. Paul morning newspaper on Aug. 29, 1958:

"In addition, city officials are considering the possibility of enclosing an enlarged stadium within a huge 'dome' roof, to permit play regardless of weather. Its financing and construction would be undertaken later, if the big league move to Midway materializes."

Just as the folks on this side of the river suspected. The idea of a dome was commandeered from St. Paul.

Patrick Reusse is a sports columnist for the St. Paul Dispatch *and* Pioneer Press.

Midway Stadium was built to lure the Brooklyn Dodgers to St. Paul. In its later years it served as a practice field for the Vikings.

Metropolitan Stadium: The Park Built for Outdoor Baseball

by JOE SOUCHERAY

Metropolitan Stadium apparently had less charm, nostalgia and history attached to it than any similar major league ball park in the country, even though, until the very last, it owned a number of distinctions that would have insured its preservation with a keener sporting public. As shocking as it might sound, open-air ball parks with natural playing surfaces are becoming as rare as bald eagles in this democracy; it is probable that fans in Boston, or New York or Chicago would lay themselves down in front of any wrecking ball out to destroy the natural order of things.

But not in Minnesota. They are tearing down the Met, and if that isn't a singular act of disrespect, it certainly reveals a great deal about our character and about the character of the Met itself, a perfectly functional and sturdy brickyard that wasn't even allowed to reach the age of 30,

when a demolition might have been justified on grounds that the joint no longer could have been trusted.

The Met went up between June, 1955 and April, 1956. The 164-acre farmland site was purchased for $478,899 by the Baseball Committee of the Minneapolis Chamber of Commerce, headed by Gerry Moore, then the Chamber's president. Bloomington was a long haul out Cedar Avenue from downtown Minneapolis. Contrary to the vague misconceptions that grew along with the park, it was not built to lure any specific major league baseball franchise to the Twin Cities. As early as 1952 Moore was simply interested in acquiring big league status for his community and he planted the same notion with Charlie Johnson, then the sports editor of the Minneapolis *Star* and *Tribune*.

Baseball was changing its face drastically during the early 1950s. In April, 1953 the National League voted to transfer the Boston Braves to Milwaukee. That autumn the St. Louis Browns became the Baltimore Orioles. There were rumblings out of New York that the Dodgers and Giants would be striking out for new territories. It was a good time to try and get a piece of the action.

The baseball committee formed by the chamber— Lyman Wakefield, Jr., Joyce Swan, Ken Dayton, William Boyer, Moore and Johnson—undertook as its initial task the building of a suitable ballyard. Moore had been told by Horace Stoneham, owner of the Giants, and Frank Lane, chairman of the major league's expansion committee, that the Twin Cities would never get major league baseball

without a major league park. It wasn't as obvious as it seemed. Even during the building of the Met and the search for a tenant, the Parade Grounds stadium was advertised as a major league facility.

To build a ball park on land in Bloomington that wasn't yet purchased, the chamber created an organization called the Minute Men to raise the necessary $4.5 million in private capital. The Minute Men fell short. As of April, 1955 they had raised just $2.2 million. An investment house that promised to handle the remaining $2.3 million cut its bond offering to $1 million. To account for the additional $1.3 million, 50 Minneapolis businessmen put their markers out in the community and produced the dough.

Ground was broken on June 20, 1955, but not before a farmer named Paul Gerhardt, who had grown onions, melons and sweet corn on the 50-acre parcel he was selling to the committee, lined up his farm machinery as a barricade along what would become the first-base line. He hadn't been paid. And he didn't start up and motor off until he received his check for $122,000.

By September an outline of the park began to appear. About the only thing that slowed construction was an explosion and fire on Feb. 26, 1956 under the grandstand along the third-base line. But the stadium opened less than two months after the fire, on April 24, 1956, featuring the Minneapolis Millers—displaced from old Nicollet Park—and Wichita in an American Association season opener.

The very same civic boosterism that has become so prominent with the domed stadium was evident in 1956 as well. Newspapers called the opening "The Miracle of 78th Street." A record crowd for a Millers' opener, 18,366, turned out in 45-degree weather. They were introduced to only the barest stadium—the main three-decked grandstand was complete and wrapped from third base to first. But the continuation of the two decks along the right field line was not undertaken until 1961. There were just temporary bleachers along the third-base line and nothing in the reaches of the outfield except an unobstructed view of the adjoining agricultural institutions. That remained one of the Met's distinctions until the end: From no other big league ball park in America could a working farm field be seen.

In exchange for a reduction in their rent, the Vikings built the left field pavilion in time for the 1965 season when the Twins hosted the All Star game and later found themselves in the World Series against the Dodgers. But that is to rush the story. The history of the Met can easily be distinguished from the history of its tenants, the Twins,

Norm McGrew, general manager of the Greater Minneapolis Chamber of Commerce, right, and Chet Roan, former manager of Metropolitan Stadium, were instrumental in the building of Met Stadium in 1955.

Vikings and Kicks, along with the Beatles and a variety of other one-shot artists.

For five seasons, while the Met was tinkered with and expanded, it was home almost exclusively to the Millers. There was always speculation that the Met would become home to the New York Giants, as the Millers were a Horace Stoneham property. But Stoneham deserted New York for San Francisco and it was only then that Minnesota began to woo Calvin Griffith out of Washington. Calvin wasn't making any dough in D.C, and therefore was a very good prospect for wooing. After five years of negotiations between the Minneapolis Baseball Committee and the Griffiths, the American League voted on Oct. 26, 1960, to award an expansion franchise to Los Angeles, move the Senators to Minnesota and replace the Senators with another expansion franchise.

The second, official Met opener then was April 21, 1961, when the new Twins hosted the new Washington Senators. On this occasion 24,606 clients turned out, with

First Millers Lineup at the Met
(vs. Wichita, April 24, 1956)

CF Billy Wells
2B Joe Amalfitano
1B Bill White
RF Bill Taylor
3B Ozzie Virgil
LF Willie Kirkland
C   Jake Jenkins
SS Eddie Bressoud
P   Jim Constable

temperatures in the mid-50s and strong westerly winds. If dealing with weather was one of the excuses for dumping the Met, it is ironic that opening-day attendance increased at the end of the Met's tenure along with a general trend of warmer and warmer opening-day temperatures until a record in one department, 89 degrees, was set on April 22, 1980 and a record in the other, 42,658, was established on April 9, 1981.

Inconsistent and sometimes drastic weather at the Met was another distinction worth preserving, particularly for the Vikings. No other team in the National Football League developed such a legend of cold weather invincibility, a legend that will disappear indoors.

Admittedly, the Met was never a candidate for architectural citation, what with its extremely poor sight lines for football and soccer and the general rundown appearance it assumed in its dotage. But it's easy now to forget how unusual the Met was, at least in 1956. The stadium was of cantilever design, no posts, poles or pillars held anything up or obstructed any views. Cantilever construction was considered innovative in 1956, when the Met was called the last word in baseball facilities.

The final baseball game ever played there was on Sept. 30, 1981. It was played in a light rain, a condition similar to that of the major league opener 21 seasons earlier. Between those rains an entire generation was introduced to professional sports at the Met. That it was all outdoors will stand as the Met's lone heritage.

Joe Soucheray is a sports columnist for the Minneapolis Tribune *and the author of* Once There Was a Ball Park, *a nostalgic tribute to Metropolitan Stadium.*

Twins Seating Chart

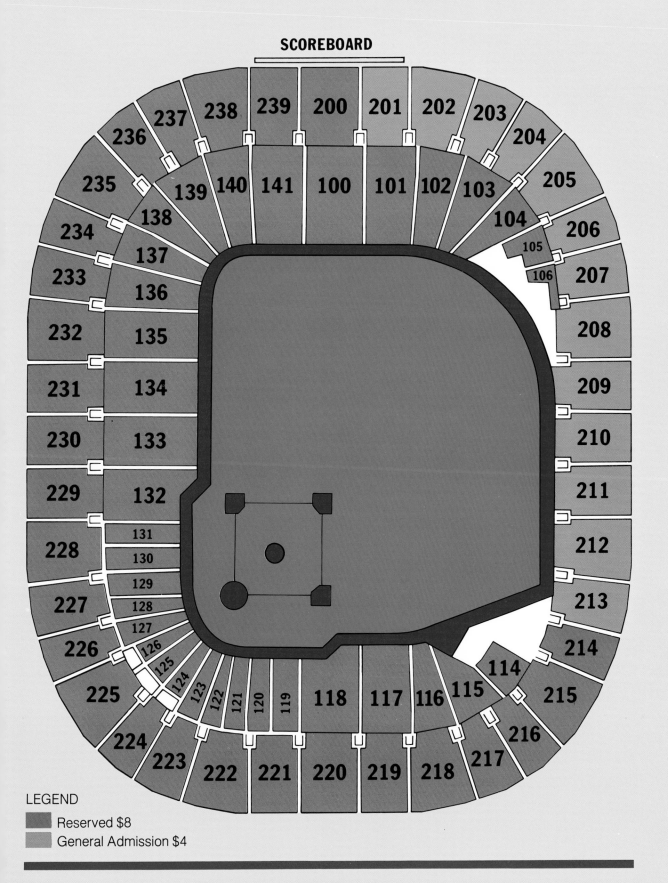

SCOREBOARD

237 238 239 200 201 202 203
236 204
235 139 140 141 100 101 102 103 205
234 138 104 206
233 137 105
232 136 106 207
231 135 208
230 134 209
229 133 210
228 132 211
131 212
227 130 213
226 129 214
225 128
224 127 114 215
223 126 115 216
222 125 116 217
221 124 117
220 123 118 218
219 122 219
121
120
119

LEGEND

Reserved $8

General Admission $4

Parking for Metrodome Events

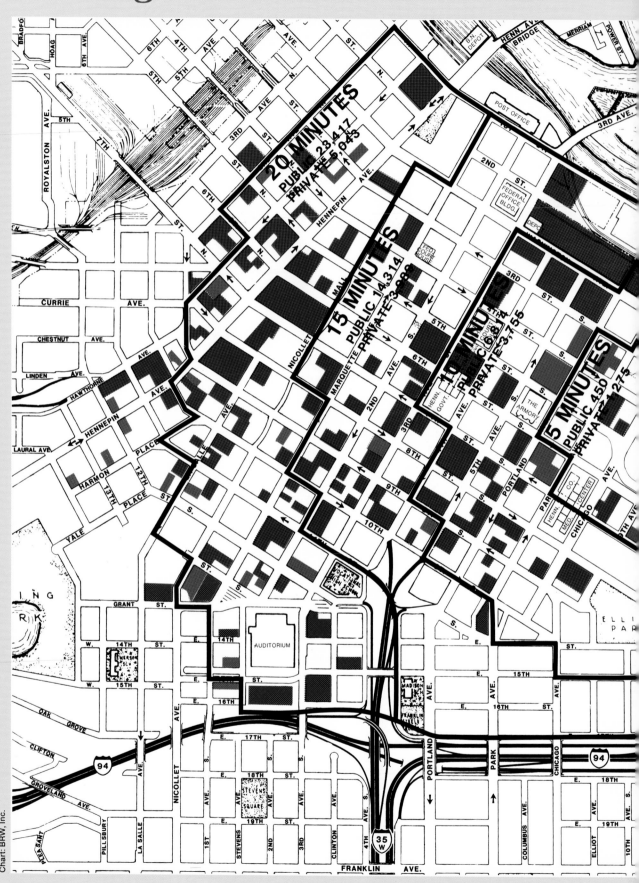

LEGEND

◼ General Public Parking

◼ Private Parking
(may not be available to public on all dates)

Walking Time Zones

Vikings Seating Chart

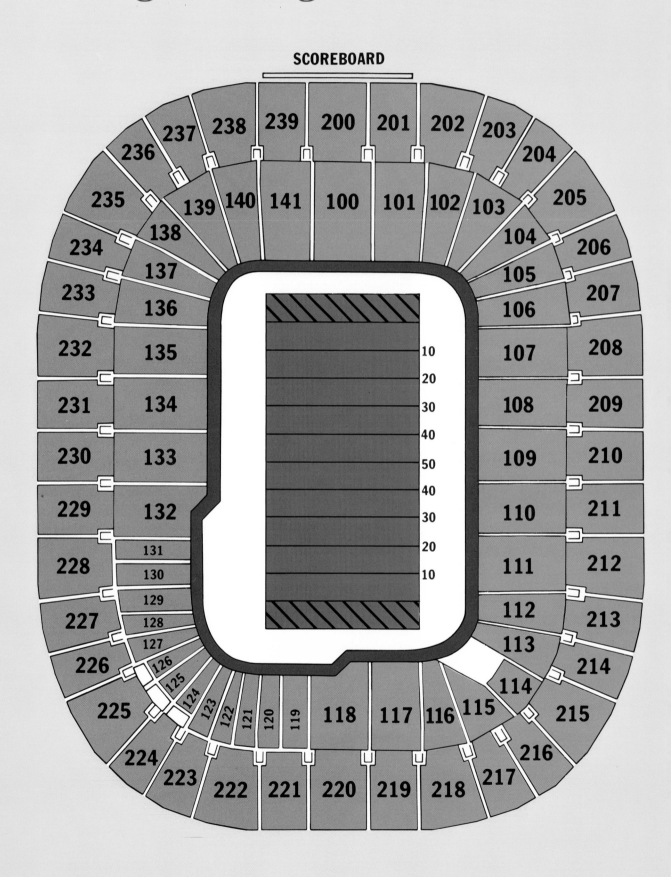

How to Get to the Metrodome

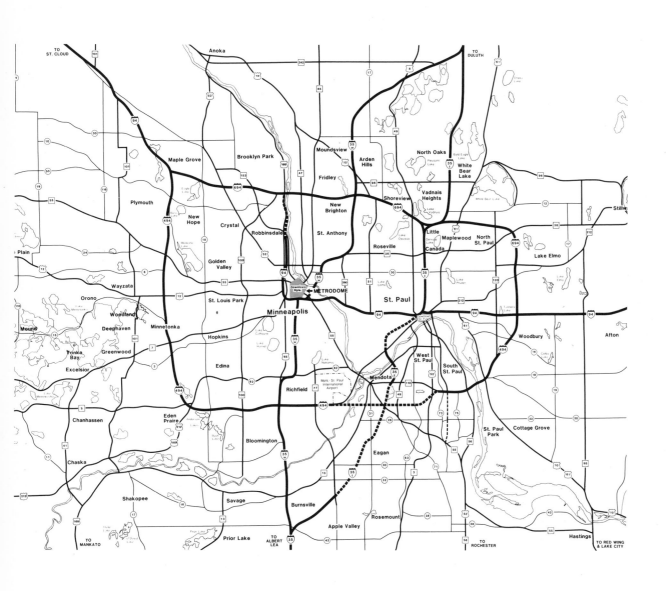

Domed Stadiums in Other Cities

▲ **ASTRODOME**
LOCATION: Houston, Texas
COST: $38 million
COMPLETED: 1965
SEATING CAPACITY: 53,000
PRINCIPAL TENANTS: Houston Oilers Football
Houston Astros Baseball

▼ **SUPERDOME**
LOCATION: New Orleans, Louisiana
COST: $168.0 million
COMPLETED: 1975
SEATING CAPACITY: 72,000
PRINCIPAL TENANTS: New Orleans Saints Football

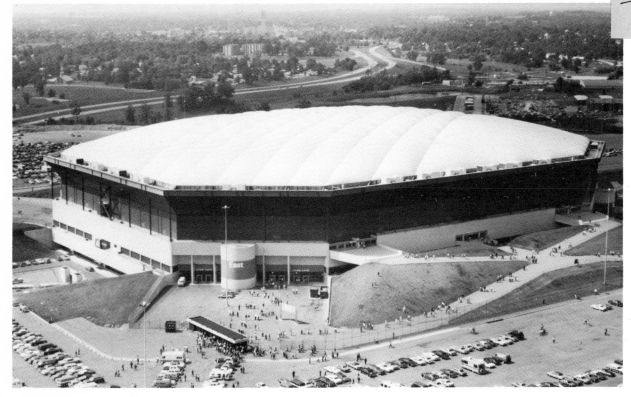

▲ SILVERDOME

LOCATION: Pontiac, Michigan
COST: $43.5 million
COMPLETED: 1975
SEATING CAPACITY: 80,638
PRINCIPAL TENANTS: Detroit Lions Football

▼ KING DOME

LOCATION: Seattle, Washington
COST: $64.0 million
COMPLETED: 1976
SEATING CAPACITY: 65,000
PRINCIPAL TENANTS: Seattle Seahawks Baseball
                   Seattle Mariners Football

Halsey Hall Recalls: His Favorite Saints and Millers

Halsey Hall, as much as any other person, was identified with the development of sports in the Twin Cities area. For well over 50 years he broadcast and wrote about amateur and professional sports in the Upper Midwest.

Shortly before his death in 1977 Halsey put down his thoughts on a number of the greatest baseball players in Minneapolis and St. Paul during the decades of the '30s, '40s and '50s.

At the time of his death, just as plans were being developed for the Metrodome, there was a large expression of public sentiment in favor of naming the Metrodome for Hall.

The 21 Halsey Hall baseball cards reproduced here are available through the mail by sending a check for $3 to Olde Cards, Inc., 1760 19th St. NW., St. Paul, MN 55112.

TED WILLIAMS

Ted Williams playing at Nicollet Park. Wouldn't you think he'd hit 80 home runs? Ted hit 43, I think it was. Of course, he led the league in that and in hitting, RBI's, runs scored, total bases and walks. Not a bad year for a twenty-year-old kid!

Williams hit two inside-the-park home runs that year in Louisville. That wasn't done again until Richie Allen of the White Sox did it against the Twins at the Met.

But Ted was temperamental. Donie Bush went to owner Mike Kelly once and said, 'Mike, that kid's gotta go or I go.' Mike said, 'Well, we're gonna miss you, Donie.' That was the end of that!

But what a natural hitter.

Born August 30, 1918, San Diego, California. The young outfielder played for the Millers in 1938. Batted left but threw right-handed.

HALSEY HALL

"In case you never heard a Minnesota Twins baseball broadcast, or never checked out who was who in the sports pages of Minnesota's newspapers for a half-century plus, or, in case you never heard him holler "Holy Cow" and regale crowds at somewhere between 600 and 700 sports banquets—well—just in case you've done none of these things—the man's name is Halsey Hall."

Terrence J. Murphy
Mpls. Tribune staff writer

This man (broadcaster, *Mpls. Tribune* sportswriter, you name it) who was so much a part of the sports scene in the Upper Midwest these last fifty-eight years, passed away December 30, 1977 at the age of seventy-nine.

For millions of sports fans, countless friends and ordinary guys like us who enjoy talking baseball, this warm, humorous, much-loved man cannot be replaced.

Born May 23, 1898, New York, New York.
Batted 1.000

NICOLLET PARK

Located in Minneapolis, Minnesota, at Nicollet Avenue and Thirty-first Street, it had a seating capacity of 10,000. Distances from plate to fences: left field, 336 feet; center field, 435 feet; right field, 279 feet. The park was razed in the late fifties to make way for a bank.

Jack Cassini

Willie Mays

JACK CASSINI

Jack Cassini played one of the greatest tricks in the history of baseball. He was with Memphis and the pitcher for the other side was one of these guys with a terrific windup . . . you know, like Pascual, Sandy Koufax, Tiant . . . He bends w-a-a-y back. And of course, every pitcher sighting a hitter gets a bead. It might be the visor of his cap, it might be his shoulder, and that's his bead.

Well, Cassini's batting with the winning run on third. He's a right-handed hitter, and as the pitcher goes into his wild windup, Cassini turns around. Now he stays in the right-handed batters' box, but his rump is toward home plate. The pitcher lets fly and of course it's a wild pitch by three feet and Memphis wins the ball game.

Only Cassini could think of that.

Born October 26, 1931, Dearborn, Michigan. Jack played second base and was right-handed all the way.

WILLIE MAYS

Mays and Clemente had the greatest arms I ever saw in baseball. You know, when Ted Williams would have batting practice, the other club would stop whatever it was doing to watch. Well, they used to stop and watch Willie in outfield practice because of his arm.

Willie might've broken every record in the history of the Association. He was hitting .477 after 38 games and leading the league in everything when Leo Durocher (managing the Giants) called Willie on the phone. Leo says, 'Willie, come on up!' 'I don't want to, Mr. D,' says Willie. Leo asks, 'What are ya hitting?' Willie answers, '.474.' There's dead silence for about 15 seconds—now that's a heck of a long silence when you're on the phone. Leo then roars, 'You get your $!&*#% on the first plane for New York!' So up he went, and the rest is history.

There's been only one like Willie.

Born May 6, 1931, Westfield, Alabama.

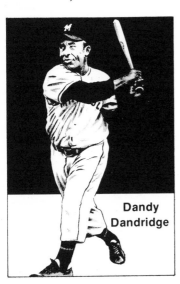

Dandy Dandridge

Campy Campanella

DANDY DANDRIDGE

All-time third baseman in the American Association, certainly. I wouldn't feel ashamed of myself if I ranked him with Brooks Robinson, or Ozzie Bleuge or Pie Traynor.

He always threw a man out by a step-and-a-half. I don't care how fast a man was, or if a guy was so slow he looked like he was pushing a safe to first base, Dandy would manage to stall and throw him out by a step-and-a-half . . . it was uncanny.

Hennesy or Gilmore was covering the Saints and we had been raving about Dandridge and somebody hit a ball down there and Dandy lobbed it over and, 'Ha, is that the great Dandridge?' I said, 'Just a minute.' Sure enough, here comes a bunt and zip, the guy's out by . . . you guessed it—a step-and-a-half on a perfect bunt.

A great ballplayer . . . good hitter, good fielder and good runner. He ran like a crab with those bowlegs, but oh, he could scamper.

Born August 31, 1919, Richmond, Virginia.

CAMPY CAMPANELLA

When he joined the Dodgers in 1948, Rickey told him, 'You're the best catcher we have, but I'd like you to go to Saint Paul. Our club there needs help.' He went and I think he hit something like eleven homers in eleven games. After about 35 games, Bruce Edwards was injured and Campy was recalled. The rest is history.

He always looked overweight . . . but you know, you can't be out of shape if you catch 300 games a year, including four games in one day, which he did in his days in the Negro leagues.

A great catcher. A tremendous hitter—I think he holds the record for catchers in homers and runs batted in for one year, 1953, I believe it was. He hit 41 homers and drove in 142 runs.

It's no wonder he'd be in the Hall of Fame . . . you could see it even then.

Born November 19, 1921, Philadelphia, Pa.

Boon Haas

Dave Barnhill

Pearidge Day

Tom Sheehan

Joe Hauser

Harley Davidson

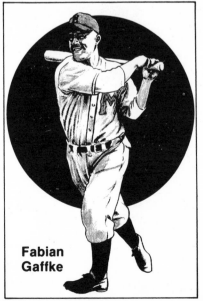

Fabian Gaffke

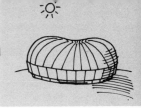

Oscar Roettger

George Stumpf

Babe Barna

Hoyt Wilhelm

Buzz Arlett

Ray Moore

Rube Benton

How Major League Baseball Came to Minnesota

by CHARLES O. JOHNSON

If anyone wants a back-breaking job that will offer many frustrating experiences, try organizing a committee with the No. 1 assignment of getting a major league sports franchise for any new area.

Scores of our more civic- and sports-minded individuals in the Twin Cities spent seven full years on such a chore. They were rebuffed at every turn, and the wonder is that they didn't throw in the sponge somewhere along the way.

It's history that Jerry Moore, as president of the Greater Minneapolis Chamber of Commerce, started the ball rolling at a luncheon attended by me (I was then executive sports editor of The Minneapolis *Star* and *Tribune*), Moore and Norm McGrew, the chamber's general manager, in late 1952. Moore asked me to inquire at the baseball commissioner's office in New York about possible expansion plans, and I did that later in the year.

Before the local committee could swing into action, the then Boston Braves of the National League, owned by Lou Perini, got permission to move to Milwaukee, which had a new park ready for occupancy. This unexpected development encouraged the Twin Cities committee with the hope that some other unhappy club owner might also like to move.

By midsummer of 1953 it became quite evident that Bill Veeck, as the boss man of the St. Louis Browns, wanted to follow the Braves' lead and invade a new area. He had his sights on Baltimore.

All summer the Twin Cities committee was in contact with Veeck, trying to get him to consider this area for his new home. He didn't even give the committee the courtesy of coming up for a visit. Under pressure, Bill finally sent his old pal of the Harlem Globetrotters, Abe Saperstein, to look over plots of ground that would be suitable for a major league park. Abe was impressed, but Veeck decided it was Baltimore or no place.

What happened to the Browns was settled at an American League meeting that dragged out for several days in New York. All cities interested in getting the Browns were given a hearing at this session. This included the Twin Cities. But at that time the Twin Cities had so little to offer that the presentation lacked strength.

The Twin Cities had one enthusiastic booster for them at this gathering of owners. He was Clark ("the Old Fox") Griffith. He pointed out what a fine baseball area we had and said we deserved a franchise.

While pleading our case with Veeck, we arranged to have the baseball stadium at the Parade Grounds in Minneapolis enlarged to seat 20,000 if a club would move to the Twin Cities. This would be used while a major league facility was to be built. We offered a guarantee of 800,000 fans for the season.

Then the local campaigners turned their attention to Horace Stoneham's New York Giants. Stoneham's club wasn't drawing well. He owned the Minneapolis Millers, and his general manager here, Rosy Ryan, kept telling his boss what a gold mine he would have if he ever moved out here. No response.

On July 4, 1954, the Twin Cities got their first break. Louis Jacobs and his attorney, representing the largest creditors of Connie Mack and the Philadelphia Athletics, came to Minneapolis. We huddled in a super hush-hush meeting.

This group said they could deliver the Athletics' franchise to the Twin Cities if the Twin Cities committee could raise $1.6 million as down payment on the overall cost of a $3.2 million obligation. They would keep the A's in Philadelphia until a stadium could be built here.

The next morning this offer was presented to the local baseball committee. But we were in the thick of a drive to raise private money to build a stadium. "We must do that first," the chairman announced. "Once we get the stadium, we'll make our move for a team."

The late Arnold Johnson was going the limit in trying to buy the Athletics and move them to Kansas City. However, some of the owners in the American League felt the Twin Cities offered a much brighter business future. The offer to the Twin Cities was renewed, but only $800,000 of the needed $1.6 million down payment could be raised here.

Arnold Johnson got the Athletics, rebuilt Kansas City's Municipal Stadium and opened the 1955 season there.

In the summer of 1955, with construction of Metropolitan Stadium underway, the Minneapolis *Star* and *Tribune* directed me to visit as many of the major league baseball owners as possible to point out the advantages of big league baseball in the Upper Midwest.

I was greeted cordially in every city, but I received no promises of franchise switching. Much of my time was spent with Stoneham in New York, but he wasn't ready to commit himself to leaving Broadway.

One of my stops was in Washington to chat with the late Clark Griffith, who had adopted Calvin and his sister Thelma (Haynes).

Funny thing, but Calvin was on hand in his uncle's office when I had a six-hour session with Clark. No promises were made by Clark, but he said the Twin Cities deserved a franchise. "They'll never move the Senators out of Washington as long as I'm alive," he told me. When he died later that year, majority ownership of the club passed to Calvin and Thelma.

As Metropolitan Stadium was finished in 1956, the search for a franchise became desperate. Finally, it was decided to have a showdown with Stoneham and his Giants. A select committee headed by E.W. Boyer, then president of the chamber, made a concrete offer to the Giants on rental, concessions and other matters. Horace listened attentively, but he gave no indication of his interests.

The very next day, Stoneham met with the mayor of San Francisco. He was offered the greatest giveaway deal that any club owner had ever received. He didn't announce it immediately, but a little later in 1956 he joined Walter O'Malley and his Brooklyn Dodgers in moving their teams to the West Coast for the 1957 season.

This unexpected development didn't completely discourage the Twin Cities committee, but it did limit its field of activities. Through 1957 and 1958, negotiations continued with Calvin Griffith as well as the owners of the Cleveland Indians.

Cleveland was having attendance problems. At the 1957 World Series in Milwaukee, three representatives from Minneapolis and St. Paul met secretly with Nate Dolan, majority owner of the Indians. It was quite evident that the Indians wanted to move, but they had a long rental contract with the city of Cleveland for Municipal Stadium. The owners had other commitments in Cleveland that made them reluctant to seek permission from the league to move. There were more sessions with these people, but little progress.

Early in 1958, it was apparent that Washington was in the shakiest financial position of any team in the major leagues and the most likely to move.

There were many sessions with Calvin Griffith. They came to a head before the 1958 All-Star game in Baltimore. The Washington prexy finally agreed that he would ask his fellow owners at this mid-summer meeting for permission to move to the Twin Cities. However, much to our dismay, he was talked out of making the request.

Through the rest of 1958 and 1959 the negotiations with Calvin continued. Several times he was on the verge of asking permission to move here, but each time he was talked out of making his request at the last minute.

In the meantime, the Continental League was organizing. It was so close to becoming a reality that both the American and National Leagues began to worry. Both had agreed to expand by at least two franchises each, but neither had set a date.

The Boston Red Sox had moved their Triple A franchise to Minneapolis and the Met. Local baseball boosters arranged exhibition games with major league teams, including one with Washington. Visiting clubs were guaranteed $10,000 each to play here. These promotions were most profitable and helped ease the financial load of the bond payments.

The big break for Minnesota and the Upper Midwest came unexpectedly the night of Oct. 25, 1960, on the eve of a meeting of the American League club owners.

Jerry Moore, Bill Boyer, Wheelock Whitney, Gordon Ritz and I were on hand in New York. Moore and Griffith were in several conferences. Calvin indicated that his move to the Twin Cities could happen the next day. He told Moore that he would have to have financial help from the Minnesota group to make the change. He asked for $250,000 in moving expenses, financial help from the banks, plus a guarantee of a 40,000-seat stadium and 750,000 paid fans for each of the first three years.

After Griffith's request, the committee met far into the wee hours of the morning. The members finally agreed to meet all of Griffith's requests and told him of their decision before Calvin's deadline of 8:45 a.m., October 26.

The Twin Cities, Los Angeles and Dallas-Fort Worth were the three leading contenders for two expanded franchises if the American League decided to go to 10 teams.

Los Angeles was considered a cinch because the American League wanted to challenge the National League on the Pacific Coast. Dallas-Fort Worth representatives thought they were cinches to get the other, because they had strong backing from Del Webb, one of the owners of the Yankees, and other magnates.

In fact, the Texans were so sure of themselves that they were offering their sympathies to the Minneapolis delegation (St. Paul had no one in New York).

The league meeting went on all morning. There wasn't even a break for lunch. Along about 3:30 p.m. it was announced that League President Joe Cronin had called a news conference.

Moore and I were the only members of the local committee around at the time. We took our places in the meeting room and were startled to hear Cronin say:

"The American League has voted today to add two teams to active membership with the start of the 1961 season. One franchise will go to Los Angeles. Calvin Griffith will move his Washington Senators to the Twin Cities of Minneapolis and St. Paul. A new franchise has been awarded to Washington under local ownership."

I rushed for a long-distance telephone to get the word to the *Star* and *Tribune*. Moore stayed in the meeting room to get additional details.

A sight to behold was the Texas delegation, which had been so certain of getting a franchise They were not only disappointed, but hostile. They thought they had been double-crossed, but they weren't sure by whom.

Boyer, Ritz and Whitney were rounded up in New York. And then a wild scene followed in the Griffith apartment. Telephones were ringing all over the place. Some calls were from Calvin's family in Washington. They were surprised by the move, as he had kept his plans to himself. The lines from Minneapolis and St. Paul to New York were swamped. Radio and television equipment soon filled the suite, and the news spread over the country that the Twin Cities' seven-year search for major league baseball had ended.

(Charles O. Johnson, veteran Minneapolis newspaper reporter and editor, was executive sports editor of the Minneapolis Star *and* Tribune *when major league baseball and football came to this area. He is now retired and living in Minneapolis.)*

Calvin Griffith: Not Even My Family Knew We Were Moving to Minnesota

by DAVE MONA

Calvin Griffith's first memories of Minnesota's efforts to secure a major league baseball franchise date back to visits by Charles Johnson, sports editor of the Minneapolis *Star* and *Tribune*, to Calvin's uncle, Clark Griffith.

"I used to see Charlie visiting my uncle," Calvin recalled, "and I'd think to myself, 'There goes that poor guy again. Talk about a lost cause.'

"After Charlie would leave I'd talk to Clark, and he said he would always tell Charlie to be patient. . .that this area's best bet of getting a major league franchise was through expansion." And since the major leagues hadn't expanded in the 20th century, the odds in favor of major league baseball coming to Minnesota seemed remote back in the early 1950s.

While Clark Griffith ran the Washington Senators there was no chance the team would leave the nation's capital, and the baseball Hall of Famer would have preferred the team remain in Washington under the direction of his adopted son, Calvin.

"I remember Clark telling me that if it was possible I should keep the club in Washington," Calvin said, "but he told me if the day ever came when I couldn't make money at it, there was no law anywhere in the baseball books to keep me from moving."

When Clark Griffith died in 1955 and management of the franchise passed to Calvin, the betting in Washington sports circles was that young Calvin would unload the team within a year.

"My uncle didn't bring me up to be a quitter," Calvin said. "He raised me to be a fighter. Besides, franchises weren't worth much in those days. Hell, the property we owned was probably worth more than the entire franchise."

Soon after the death of his uncle, Calvin received regular visits from delegations wooing the Senators with promises of profit potential far beyond the scope of anything the team had been able to achieve in Washington.

The Los Angeles and San Francisco delegations told of population shifts and the possibilities of jet transportation and coaxial cables for coast-to-coast television coverage. The Dallas-Fort Worth crowd moved in with a hard sell and big dollars, and a steady stream of Twin Cities people stopped by to pay their respects.

Charlie Johnson, Bill Boyer, H.P. Skoglund, Gerry Moore, Wheelock Whitney and Gordon Ritz regularly made the rounds of potential league movers, and also spent time angling for a franchise in the about-to-be-launched Continental League under Branch Rickey.

"It was pretty much assumed in baseball circles that if anyone was going to move to the Twin Cities it would be the New York Giants because they'd been talking to this area for a long time and the Minneapolis Millers were their top farm club," Griffith said.

Because he didn't want to waste his time on a dead issue, Griffith sought out New York Giants' owner Horace Stoneham in late 1956 to ask him if he planned to move the Giants to Minnesota.

"He told me, 'Calvin, I just don't know what I'm going to do.' The next thing you know I read in the paper one day the Giants are going to move along with the Dodgers to the West Coast. I honestly didn't know anything about that before most baseball fans. The National League was a whole nother world."

With the Giants out of the picture, the major league rumor mill was placing other franchises in the Twin Cities.

"I heard it was going to be Cleveland," Griffith said, "and then I heard it was the Chicago White Sox."

About that time the Minnesota delegation paid another call on Griffith, inviting him personally to come out and see the new Metropolitan Stadium.

"They offered me a $10,000 guarantee to play an exhibition game against the Philadelphia Phillies," Griffith said. "I knew we weren't making any money at the time and I thought, 'What the hell. . .$10,000 is more money than I take in any place but New York.' So I said ok."

That was in 1958 and Griffith stayed for an entire week while local business and community leaders began to draw pictures of the good life Minnesota had to offer.

"Chet Roan took me everywhere," Griffith chuckled. "He only let me out of his sight to go to bed. I think we hit every good restaurant in town.

"I remember that we went out to the old Cedric's at 50th and Hwy. 100 in Edina on a Saturday. Roan made sure we had a table that looked out on Hwy. 100.

"'See all those cars with boats behind them?' he said. 'These people are starved for something to do for recreation on the weekends. They work hard all week and

Minnesota Twins President and Owner Calvin Griffith.

on the weekend they could all be out there at Met Stadium watching your team play.'"

Deep down, Griffith admits now he knew he was being hyped, but after the constant abuse he says he took at the hands of the Washington news media, the flattery felt good. "It inflated my ego," he said. "It made me feel wanted. They wanted to get a commitment out of me right then and there, but I told them to be patient . . . that the right opportunity hadn't arisen yet."

That was not the case two years later at the American League baseball meetings after the 1960 World Series.

As usual, the Minnesota delegation was there, but the prospect of shopping in the New York stores was much more alluring than the seemingly remote possibility of any good news coming out of these meetings.

"The night before the meeting," Griffith said, "I told Charlie Johnson and Gerry Moore that there was no way we were gonna do anything the next day.

"I also did a radio tape with [WCCO's] Rollie Johnson on the possibility of moving to Minnesota, but I made him promise to destroy it if nothing happened at the meetings."

As the day began and the agendas were distributed there was no talk of expansion or franchise shifts.

"There was sort of a clique that ran things back in those days," Griffith said. "Howard Fox and I were sitting in the meeting and all of a sudden we were talking about a team in Los Angeles and, before you know it, the Los Angeles franchise is awarded to Hank Greenberg.

"I turned to Howard and said, 'Do you know what they just did? They've just expanded our league.'

"I said, 'Howard, you know, we can make it in Minneapolis/St. Paul.' So I got up and said I wanted their permission to move the franchise to Minnesota."

After a brief discussion a vote was taken and it was 5-3 against allowing the move. At that point, American League President Joe Cronin said the meeting would adjourn for lunch. As the other club leaders got up to leave, Griffith recalls telling Fox, "This means we're out of baseball. When this story gets out in Washington, they're going to kill us." Just then New York Yankees owner Dan Topping asked Griffith how serious he was about wanting to move his franchise.

"It's the most serious I've ever been in my life," Griffith replied.

"Then don't worry," Topping said. "You'll get your way."

After lunch, Topping asked to resume the discussion of the move of the Washington franchise. "We can always find someone to start another team in Washington," he said. "I want a revote."

Griffith recalls his blood ran hot as a show of hands was asked. This time the vote was 5-3 in favor of the move, and Griffith was back in baseball.

A few minutes later, Baltimore owner Joseph Iglehart said he had just realized what he had done and wanted to change his yes vote to a no vote.

"You're too late," said Cronin, who also happened to be Griffith's brother-in-law. "The team's in Minnesota now."

All that remained was to tell the world and to work out a plan for a move that hadn't even been seriously contemplated hours earlier.

After the meeting, Griffith and Fox headed straight for Griffith's suite where they met [Twin Cities sportscaster] Frank Buetel, recorder in hand. Rollie Johnson arrived seconds later.

As the room filled with media people from Minnesota and Washington, Griffith's wife returned from shopping.

"What's going on?" she asked.

"Welcome to Minnesota," someone said.

"What are you talking about?" she demanded.

Meanwhile, a golf cart was dispatched onto the back nine at Indian Springs Country Club in suburban Washington where Griffith's brothers, Sherry, Billy and Jimmy, were enjoying a round of golf.

"Calvin's moved the team to Minnesota," the messenger said.

"Calvin wouldn't do that without telling us," Sherry replied.

Looking back, Griffith calls that October day one that will live with him forever.

"If you had told me when I got up that morning that by the end of the day we'd have a baseball team in Minnesota," he said, "I'd have told you flat out you were nuts."

Minnesota Twins: Statistics

TWINS' CAREER HOME RUN LEADERS

1.	Harmon Killebrew	475
2.	Tony Oliva	220
3.	Bob Allison	211
4.	Jimmie Hall	98
5.	Don Mincher	90
6.	Larry Hisle	87
7.	Zoilo Versalles	86
8.	Earl Battey	76
9.	Rod Carew	74
10.	Rich Rollins	71
11.	Bobby Darwin	70
11.	Roy Smalley	70

TWINS' MANAGERS

	Seasons	Won	Lost	Pct.
Cookie Lavagetto	1961	25	41	.379
Sam Mele	1961-67	522	431	.548
Cal Ermer	1967-68	145	129	.529
Billy Martin	1969	97	65	.599
Bill Rigney	1970-72	208	184	.531
Frank Quilici	1972-75	280	287	.494
Gene Mauch	1976-80	378	394	.490
Johnny Goryl	1980-81	34	38	.472
Billy Gardner	1981-	30	43	.411

ALL-TIME WINNINGEST PITCHERS

Righthanders:	Seasons	Won	Lost	Pct.
Jim Perry	(1963-72)	128	90	.587
Bert Blyleven	(1970-76)	99	90	.524
Dave Goltz	(1972-79)	96	79	.549
Camilo Pascual	(1961-66)	88	57	.607
Dave Boswell	(1964-70)	67	54	.554
Lefthanders:				
Jim Kaat	(1961-73)	189	152	.554
Geoff Zahn	(1977-80)	53	53	.500
Jerry Koosman	(1979-81)	39	35	.527
Dick Stigman	(1962-65)	37	37	.500
Jim Merritt	(1965-68)	37	41	.474

YEARLY BATTING LEADERS

	Average			Home Runs		Runs Batted In	
1961	Battey	.302	Killebrew	46	Killebrew	122
1962	Rollins	.298	Killebrew	48	Killebrew	126
1963	Rollins	.307	Killebrew	45	Killebrew	96
1964	Oliva	.323	Killebrew	49	Killebrew	111
1965	Oliva	.321	Killebrew	25	Oliva	98
1966	Oliva	.307	Killebrew	39	Killebrew	110
1967	Carew	.292	Killebrew	44	Killebrew	113
1968	Oliva	.289	Allison	22	Oliva	68
1969	Carew	.332	Killebrew	49	Killebrew	140
1970	Oliva	.325	Killebrew	41	Killebrew	113
1971	Oliva	.337	Killebrew	28	Killebrew	119
1972	Carew	.318	Killebrew	26	Darwin	80
1973	Carew	.364	Darwin	18	Oliva	92
1974	Carew	.364	Darwin	25	Darwin	94
1975	Carew	.359	Ford	15	Carew	80
1976	Carew	.331	Ford	20	Hisle	96
1977	Carew	.388	Hisle	28	Hisle	119
1978	Carew	.333	Smalley	19	Ford	82
1979	Landreaux	.305	Smalley	24	Smalley	95
1980	Castino	.302	Castino	13	Castino	64
1981	Castino	.268	Smalley	7	Hatcher	37

YEARLY PITCHING LEADERS

	Victories		Earned Run Average		Strikeouts	
1961	Pascual	15-16	Pascual	3.46	Pascual	221
1962	Pascual	20-11	Kaat	3.14	Pascual	206
1963	Pascual	21-9	Pascual	2.47	Pascual	202
1964	Kaat	17-11	Kaat	3.22	Pascual	213
1965	Grant	21-7	Perry	2.63	Kaat	154
1966	Kaat	25-13	Perry	2.54	Kaat	205
1967	Chance	20-14	Merritt	2.53	Chance	220
1968	Chance	16-16	Chance	2.53	Chance	234
1969	Boswell	20-12	Perry	2.82	Boswell	190
	Perry	20-6				
1970	Perry	24-12	Perry	3.03	Hall	184
1971	Perry	17-17	Blyleven	2.82	Blyleven	224
1972	Blyleven	17-17	Corbin	2.61	Blyleven	228
1973	Blyleven	20-17	Blyleven	2.52	Blyleven	258
1974	Blyleven	17-17	Blyleven	2.66	Blyleven	249
1975	Hughes	16-14	Blyleven	3.00	Blyleven	233
1976	Campbell	17-5	Campbell	3.00	Goltz	133
1977	Goltz	20-11	Goltz	3.36	Goltz	186
1978	Goltz	15-10	Goltz	2.50	Erickson	121
1979	Koosman	20-13	Koosman	3.38	Koosman	157
1980	Koosman	16-13	Erickson	3.25	Koosman	149
1981	Redfern	9-8	Arroyo	3.93	Redfern	77

TWINS' INDIVIDUAL CAREER RECORDS

Batting and Base Running

Batting Average	Rod Carew .334
Seasons	Tony Oliva 15
Games	Harmon Killebrew 1,939
At Bats	Killebrew 6,593
Runs	Killebrew 1,047
Hits	Carew 2,085
Total Bases	Killebrew 1,616
Singles	Carew 1,616
Doubles	Oliva 329
Triples	Carew 90
Home Runs	Killebrew 475
Runs Batted In	Killebrew 1,325
Walks	Killebrew 1,321
Strike Outs	Killebrew 1,314
Stolen Bases	Carew 271
Sacrifices	Smalley 77
Sacrifice Flys	Killebrew 66
Hit By Pitch	Cesar Tovar 68

Pitching

Earned Run Average	Al Worthington 2.63
Percentage	Camilo Pascual .607
Seasons	Jim Kaat 13
Wins	Kaat 189
Losses	Kaat 152
Saves	Ron Perranoski 75
Games	Kaat 468
Starts	Kaat 422
Complete Games	Kaat 133
Shutouts	Bert Blyleven 24
Innings Pitched	Kaat 2,958
Hits Allowed	Kaat 2,927
Home Runs	Kaat 270
Strike Outs	Kaat 1,824
Walks	Kaat 694
Runs	Kaat 1,295
Earned Runs	Kaat 1,077

STANDINGS OF TWINS YEAR-BY-YEAR

Year	Won	Lost	Pct.	Position	Home Attendance
1961	70	90	.438	7	1,256,723
1962	91	71	.562	2	1,433,116
1963	91	70	.565	3	1,406,652
1964	79	83	.488	6	1,207,514
1965	102	60	.630	1	1,463,258
1966	89	73	.549	2	1,259,374
1967	91	71	.562	2	1,483,547
1968	79	83	.488	7	1,143,257
1969	97	65	.599	1	1,349,328
1970	98	64	.605	1	1,261,887
1971	74	86	.463	5	940,858
1972	77	77	.500	3	797,901
1973	81	81	.500	3	907,499
1974	82	80	.506	3	662,401
1975	76	83	.478	4	737,156
1976	85	77	.525	3	715,394
1977	84	77	.522	4	1,162,727
1978	73	89	.451	4	787,878
1979	82	80	.506	4	1,070,521
1980	77	84	.478	3	769,206
1981 (1)	17	39	.304	7	—
1981 (2)	24	29	.453	4	469,090

Bob Allison

Earl Battey

Bert Blyleven

Leo Cardenas

TWINS' PLAYER TRADES

No.	Date	Club	Received	Traded
1	6- 1-61	K.C.	Bill Tuttle, of	Reno Bertoia, 3b
				Paul Giel, p
2	6- 1-61	Milw.	Billy Martin, 2b	Billy Consolo, ss
3	6-14-61	N.Y.	Danny McDevitt, p	Billy Gardner, 2b
4	1-30-62	Cin.	Jerry Zimmerman, c	Dan Dobbek, of
5	4- 2-62	Clev.	Vic Power, 1b	Pedro Ramos, p
			Dick Stigman, p	
6	5-29-62	L.A. (AL)	Jim Donohue, p	Don Lee, p
7	8-20-62	Clev.	Ruben Gomez, p	Jackie Collum, p
				Georges Maranda, p
8	5- 2-63	Clev.	Jim Perry, p	Jack Kralick, p
9	6-11-64	L.A. (AL)	Frank Kostro, of	Lenny Green, of
				Vic Power, 1b
10	6-15-64	Clev.	Jim Grant, p	George Banks, 3b
				Lee Stange, p
11	10-15-64	Wash.	Ken Retzer, c	Joe McCabe, c
12	12- 4-64	Cin.	Cesar Tovar, of	Gerry Arrigo, p
13	4- 6-66	Bos.	Russ Nixon, c	Jose Calero, 1b
			Chuck Schilling, 2b	Dick Stigman, p
14	12- 2-66	Cal.	Dean Chance, p	Pete Cimino, p
			Jackie Hernandez, ss	Jimmie Hall, of
				Don Mincher, 1b
15	12- 3-66	Wash.	Ron Kline, p	Bernie Allen, 2b
				Camilo Pascual, p
16	11-28-67	L.A.	Bob Miller, p	Jim Grant, p
			Ron Perranoski, p	Zoilo Versalles, ss
			John Roseboro, c	
17	12- 2-67	Pitt.	Bob Oliver, 1b	Ron Kline, p
18	11-21-68	Cin.	Leo Cardenas, ss	Jim Merritt, p
19	7- 4-69	Chi. (AL)	Cotton Nash, 1b	Jerry Crider, p
20	7- 8-69	Sea.	Darrell Brandon, p	Ron Clark, 3b
21	12-12-69	Clev.	Luis Tiant, p	Dean Chance, p
			Stan Williams, p	Bob Miller, p
				Graig Nettles, 3b
				Ted Uhlaender, of
22	3-21-70	Wash.	Brant Alyea, of	Joe Grzenda, p
				Charley Walters, p
23	10-20-70	St. L.	Sal Campisi, p	Herman Hill, of
			Jim Kennedy, ss	Bob Wissler, of
24	3-29-71	Det.	Mike Adams, of	Bill Zepp, p
			Art Clifford, p	
25	7- 8-71	Milw.	Phil Roof, c	Paul Ratliff, c
26	9- 1-71	St. L.	Dan Ford, p	Stan Williams, p
			Fred Rico, of	
27	10-22-71	L.A.	Bob Darwin, of	Paul Powell, of
28	11-30-71	Cal.	Dave LaRoche, p	Leo Cardenas, ss

ALL-STAR GAME PLAYERS

Bob Allison, of, 1b	1963-64
Earl Battey, c	1962-63-65-66
Bert Blyleven, p	1973
Leo Cardenas, ss	1971
Rod Carew, 2b, 1b	1967-68-69-70-71-72-73-74-75-76-77-78
Dean Chance, p	1967
Doug Corbett, p	1981
Jim Grant, p	1965
Jimmie Hall, of	1964-65
Larry Hisle, of	1977

29	12- 3-71	Cin.	Wayne Granger, p	Tom Hall, p
30	4- 7-72	Cin.	Greg Garrett, p	Pete Hamm, p
31	10-31-72	N.Y. (AL)	Dan Walton, of	Rick Dempsey, c
32	11-29-72	St. L.	John Cumberland, p	Wayne Granger, p
			Larry Hisle, of	
33	11-30-72	Phil.	Joe Lis, 1b	Cesar Tovar, of
			Ken Reynolds, p	
			Ken Sanders, p	
34	11-30-72	Chi. (NL)	Joe Decker, p	Dave LaRoche, p
			Bill Hands, p	
			Bob Maneely, p	
35	3-27-73	Det.	Danny Fife, p	Jim Perry, p
36	3-28-73	Milw.	Mike Ferraro, 3b	Ken Reynolds, p
37	10-27-73	K.C.	Tom Burgmeier, p	Ken Gill, p
38	10-27-73	L.A.	Jim Fairey, of	Charlie Manuel, of
39	12- 6-73	Chi. (NL)	Randy Hundley, c	George Mitterwald, c
40	5- 4-74	N.Y. (AL)	Mike Pazik, p	Dick Woodson, p
41	8-19-74	Oak.	Pat Bourque, 1b	Jim Holt, 1b
42	10-23-74	Oak.	Dan Ford, of	Pat Bourque, 1b
			Dennis Myers, p	
43	6-14-75	Milw. . :	John Briggs, of	Bob Darwin, of
44	10-24-75	Phil.	Larry Cox, c	Sergio Ferrer, ss
45	12-23-75	L.A.	Bob Randall, 2b	Danny Walton, of
46	6- 1-76	Tex.	Mike Cubbage, 3b	Bert Blyleven, p
			Jim Gideon, p	Danny Thompson, ss
			Bill Singer, p	
			Roy Smalley, ss	
47	12- 4-78	Cal.	Danny Goodwin, c	Dan Ford, of
			Ron Jackson, 1b	
48	12- 8-78	N.Y. (NL)	Jerry Koosman, p	Greg Field, p
				Jesse Orosco, p
49	2- 3-79	Cal.	Dave Engle, c	Rod Carew, 1b
			Paul Hartzell, p	
			Brad Havens, p	
			Ken Landreaux, of	
50	2-12-79	Bos.	Dave Coleman, of	Larry Wolfe, 3b
51	4- 2-79	Chi. (AL)	John Verhoeven, p	John Sutton, p
52	12- 6-79	Phil.	Pete Mackanin, 2b	Paul Thormodsgard, p
53	12- 6-79	Balt.	Tom Chism, 1b	Dan Graham, 3b
54	12- 8-80	S.D.	Chuck Baker, ss	Dave Edwards, of
55	12-12-80	Sea.	Byron McLaughlin, p	Willie Norwood, of
56	3-30-81	L.A.	Mickey Hatcher, of	Ken Landreaux, of
			Kelly Snider, 1b	
			Matt Reeves, p	
57	8-22-81	Det.	Tim Corcoran, 1b	Ron Jackson, 1b
58	8-30-81	Chi. (AL)	Randy Johnson, of	Jerry Koosman, p
			Ivan Mesa, ss	
			Ron Perry, 3b	

Rod Carew

Dean Chance

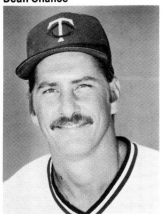

Doug Corbett

Jim Grant

| Jim Kaat, p . . . . .1962-66 |
| Harmon Killebrew, 3b, 1b, of .1961-63-64-65-66-67-68-69-70-71 |
| Ken Landreaux, of . . . . .1980 |
| Tony Oliva, of . . . . .1964-65-66-67-69-70-71 |
| Camilo Pascual, p . . . . .1961-62-64 |
| Jim Perry, p . . . . .1970-71 |
| Rich Rollins, 3b . . . . .1962 |
| John Roseboro, c . . . . .1969 |
| Roy Smalley, ss . . . . .1979 |
| Zoilo Versalles, ss . . . . .1963-65 |
| Butch Wynegar, c . . . . .1976-77 |

Jimmie Hall

Larry Hisle

Jim Kaat

Harmon Killebrew

Ken Landreaux

Tony Oliva

Camilo Pascual

Jim Perry

Rich Rollins

John Roseboro

Roy Smalley

Zoilo Versalles

Butch Wynegar

Harmon Killebrew moved with the Washington Senators to Minnesota in 1961 and, for more than a decade, terrorized American League pitching with his classic home run swing.

Memories of Metropolitan Stadium, clockwise from center left: A home run scramble on a hot July day; Twins mascot Twinkie; owner Calvin Griffith in his ground-floor office at the Met; the view from the left field corner; what grass?; Harmon Killebrew; Tony Oliva.

Rod Carew was the American League's leading hitter and a perennial All-Star with the Twins in the late '60s and through most of the '70s.

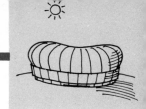

Year-by-Year with the Minnesota Twins

by BILL MORLOCK and RICK LITTLE

In their first 21 years in Minnesota the Twins won the American League championship once and the League's Western Division title twice. Here, on a year-by-year basis, is a summary of those 21 seasons played at Met Stadium.

1961

The first expansion in major League baseball since 1900 when the National League split to form the American and National leagues brought Minnesota its first taste of major league baseball. Calvin Griffith brought his cellar-dwelling Senators from Washington to Met Stadium. As Twins, the team traveled north from spring training to battle with the Yankees in New York with this starting lineup: Pedro Ramos-p, Earl Battey-c, Harmon Killebrew-1b, Ted Lepcio-2b, Reno Bertoia-3b, Zoilo Versalles-ss, Jim Lemon-lf, Lenny Green-cf and Bob Allison-rf. God knows how, but they won 6-0 (this was the year Maris hit 61 home runs and Mantle 54). When they arrived home, a similar lineup lost the first home opener at the Met to the Washington Senators, 5-3. Seventy-four games into the season the Twins were 29-45, and their first manager, Cookie Lavagetto, was replaced by Sam Mele. To shore up the error-prone infield, Griffith traded Paul Giel and Bertoia to Kansas City for outfielder Bill Tuttle, who was promptly assigned duties as third baseman. Even adding an aging Billy Martin, brought to Minnesota in a trade with the Milwaukee Braves, didn't stop the worst fielding performance in the team's history. The pitchers set records for misery also, allowing the most walks, hits and hit batsmen in the team's history. In all, the pitchers allowed an average of 13 baserunners per game. Is it any wonder they had a team 4.28 ERA? Is it any wonder they wound up 70-90, 38 games out of first? Did that make a difference to Twins fans? No! Over a million people went to see them play, and at movies, in parks and even at symphony concerts you could see transistor radios plugged into the ears of eager new fans, trying to catch the score. Baseball was a novelty in Minnesota.

First Twins Lineup at the Met
(vs. Washington Senators, April 23, 1961)

SS	Zoilo Versalles
CF	Lenny Green
1B	Don Mincher
RF	Bob Allison
LF	Jim Lemon
C	Earl Battey
3B	Reno Bertoia
2B	Billy Gardner
P	Camilo Pascual

1962

Even Griffith must have been surprised by the Twins drive toward the pennant in the season's final week. Though the Twins lost the pennant battle, they won the season's war. The 91-71 Twins were the best Griffith team in 18 years and the first to play over .500 in a decade. Camilo Pascual became the Twins' first 20-game winner, Jim Kaat chased him with 18, but Dick Stigman, Shorty Pleis and Ray "Old Blue" Moore were stellar tossers too. The greatest pitching performance of the young Twins' history was turned in by Jack Kralick, who didn't allow the hapless Kansas City A's a hit in beating them 1-0. Questions at second and third base were answered by Bernie Allen and Rich Rollins, respectively. With the addition of Vic Power, the Twins expected to add fielding strength, but Rollins led the league's third basemen in errors, and Zoilo was second worst among shortstops. The outfield of Killebrew, Green and Allison was quick up the middle but hardly diseased with speed on the flanks. The Twins poor defense lost them the pennant even though their offense was awesome. Killebrew became the Twins' first home run and RBI king that year, and the team earned a reputation for hitting with power that stayed with them throughout the '60s. This year they were fourth in the American League with 185 homers. All eight starters were in double digits for home runs, a portent of things to come. A kid named Tony Oliva was given a brief look at season's end. He hit .444 in 9 games.

1963

Baseballs flew out of Met Stadium like marbles out of an open blender as the Twins managed to nearly duplicate their previous year's record at 91-70. How about this batting order: Versalles (10 homers), Rollins (16), Allison (35), Al home run king Killebrew (45), Al rookie record-setter Jimmie Hall (33), Battey (26), Mincher (17), Allen (9) and a pitcher. The Twins hit 225 homers, second all-time in major league history to the Yankees of '61. Pascual racked up another great 21-9 season, and Lee Stange did well at 12-5; but the rest of the rotation—Kaat, Perry and Stigman—were cumulatively 34-34. "Won't You Come In Bill Dailey" was the bullpen's song that year, and manager Mele sang it often. Dailey was 6-3 with 21 saves and a nifty 1.99 ERA. But still they didn't win the pennant. The Twins were the third worst fielders in the American League (AL), just ahead of the Senators (56-106) and the Angels (70-91) with Versalles and Rollins winning the "Most Boots" contest at each of their positions. Touted as the "singles hitter" who would balance the Twins home run attack, Oliva was given another look and hit .429. He was hitting .438 lifetime for the Twins.

1964

"Where've they been keepin' this kid?" fans yelled as they watched Tony "O" rip through American League pitchers as if they were throwing batting practice. Oliva won the American League silver bat with his .323 average, led the league in hits with 217, doubles with 43, runs scored with 109, and fell one homer short of tying Jimmie Hall's rookie record with his 32 round trippers. Obviously, he was '64

Rookie of the Year and the only reason he wasn't voted MVP was because the Twins could have finished sixth even without him. The fielding was abominable—the team tied with Boston for worst in the AL. Rollins and Versalles combined for 55 errors, only 11 fewer than the entire pennant-winning Yankee team. As if the problem lay at second base, the Twins brought up five second basemen to start the season; Bernie Allen, Bill Bethea, Bud Bloomfield, Johnny Goryl and Jim Snyder. They even traded Lenny Green and Vic Power to get another second baseman, Jerry Kindall. Kindall could field, but he hit only .196. Equally rotten was the pitching staff—
second worst record in the AL. But some slick buying and trading brought Al Worthington, Johnny Klippstein and Jim "Mudcat" Grant into the fold. It didn't help much in '64, but if you don't recognize those names in '65, you weren't paying attention. Killebrew captured his third straight home run crown with 49, leading the home run derby that resulted in 221 team homers, third on the all-time list.

1965

Champagne corks popped and the locker room cheered in celebration of Jim Kaat's 2-1 victory over Pete Richert and the Washington Senators on Sunday, Sept. 26, 1965. The Twins had won the pennant. They won because of Zoilo Versalles, the AL MVP, who led the league in at bats, runs scored, doubles and triples. They won because of Tony Oliva's .321 batting average, which brought him his second batting title. The won because of Don Mincher, who came off the bench to fill in during the pennant drive for an injured Harmon Killebrew who was hurt following a collision with Baltimore's Russ Snyder. Mudcat Grant won

21 games to lead the American League, Kaat won 18 (five in September), and the bullpen of Worthington, Klippstein, Pleis and Perry was untouchable. Even Jim Merritt and Dave Boswell contributed to the starting rotation when Pascual came up with a sore arm early in the season. The pitching staff performed brilliantly, but that wasn't too surprising because the coach that year was Johnny Sain of "Spahn and Sain and pray for rain" fame. He alone was responsible for the "new" pitching staff. And though the defense didn't improve its error count, the team placed second in the AL in double plays. The Twins won with smart pitching, a self-redeeming defense and their usual solid hitting. Ironically, they did not win with a record number of homers. By the July 11 All-Star break the Twins were five games in first. They never left that position. They didn't leave Minnesota to play in the All-Star game either. Harmon pleased the home-town sellout crowd with a blast into the left field pavilion in an American League losing effort, 6-5. The baseball gods gave their blessing to Minnesota in 1965.

WORLD SERIES-1965

The Dodgers and Twins were as unlike as their home fields. The Met had soft spongy grass on both the infield and outfield; Chavez Ravine was like slate. The Twins were slow afoot, but relied on power hitting and solid pitching, while the Dodgers relied on superlative pitching from Sandy Koufax (26-8), Don Drysdale (23-13) and Claude Osteen (15-15), the baffling switch hitting of Maury Wills, Jim Lefebvre and Junior Gilliam, and the solid defense of outfielders Ron Fairly, Lou Johnson and Willie Davis.

Pitcher Jim Kaat was mobbed by his teammates after the Twins clinched the 1965 American League pennant with a 2-1 victory over the Washington Senators.

Twins Manager Sam Mele covered his eyes as the Los Angeles Dodgers raced around the bases in the fifth game of the 1965 World Series.

Uff da! Twins Catcher Earl Battey had to leave a World Series game after he ran into a padded pipe while chasing a foul ball.

Game 1—October 6 at Met Stadium. Koufax misses the opener to attend Yom Kippur services. Grant starts against Drysdale. The Dodgers strike with Ron Fairly's homer in the second, but the Twins answer with Mincher's homer in his first trip to the plate. In the third, the Twins score 6 runs on Versalles' three-run homer, Battey's bloop single and Frank Quilici's second hit of the inning. Each team scored one more run. Final score: 8-2. Winning pitcher—Grant (1-0); losing pitcher—Drysdale (0-1).

Game 2—October 7 at Met Stadium. Koufax faces Kaat in what proves to be a pitcher's duel. Scoreless to the sixth, Oliva doubles to score Versalles from third and scores on Killebrew's subsequent single. In the seventh, with Lefebvre on third and Fairly on second, Roseboro lines a soft single to left, but Fairly holds, thinking Allison might repeat his miraculous catch in the fourth off Lefebvre's bat. In the bottom of the seventh, Versalles triples and scampers home on Ron Perranoski's wild pitch. Kaat lines a single in the eighth to knock in Allison and Mincher. Final score: 5-1. Winning pitcher—Kaat (1-0); losing pitcher—Koufax (0-1).

Game 3—October 9 at Chavez Ravine. Lefty Osteen vies against Minnesota ace Pascual. In the top of the first with Versalles on third and Killebrew on first, Killebrew breaks for second and is caught in a run-down, Versalles breaks for home but is gunned down by Wills. That is as close as Minnesota comes to scoring. Roseboro's single in the fourth knocks in Fairly and Lefebvre. The Dodgers add two more. Final score: 4-0. Winning pitcher—Osteen (1-0); losing pitcher—Pascual (0-1).

Game 4—October 10 at Chavez Ravine. Grant and Drysdale replay the first game. Grant's failure to cover first on two grounders to Mincher opens the flood gates, and an error by Versalles allows Wills to score. A Grant wild pitch allows Wes Parker to score. Parker, Killebrew and Oliva hit solo home runs to make it 3-2. The bungling continues and errors by Hall, Oliva and Quilici (failing to cover first on a sacrifice bunt) in the sixth and Lou Johnson's solo blast in the eighth end the blundering fiasco. Final score: 7-2. Winning pitcher—Drysdale (1-1); losing pitcher—Grant (1-1).

Game 5—October 11 at Chavez Ravine. Kaat and Koufax are rematched. Maury Wills' four-hit burst equals the Twins' total hitting attack. Davis, Wills, Gilliam and Johnson "run-over" the Twins. Final score: 7-0. Winning pitcher—Koufax (1-1); losing pitcher—Kaat (1-1).

Game 6—October 13 at Met Stadium. Grant, feeling "lousy," faces Osteen, whom the Twins (as a Griffith organization) have never beaten in seven tries. Allison breaks the Twins' scoring slump by cracking a homer with Battey aboard in the fourth. Grant pitches out of a bases-loaded-no-outs jam in the fifth. Allison and Quilici score on Grant's homer in the sixth. Fairly's homer in the seventh is the Dodgers' only score. Final score: 5-1. Winning pitcher—Grant (2-1); losing pitcher—Osteen (1-1).

Game 7—October 14 at Met Stadium. Koufax and Kaat meet for the third go-around. The Twins threaten in the second. Versalles takes off for second base for an easy stolen base but is returned to first when Nossek is called out for swinging and stepping on the plate, thus interfering with Roseboro's throw. In the fourth, Johnson hits a solo homer and Parker knocks in Fairly. Koufax mows down 12 Twins in a row before Killebrew singles in the ninth. Koufax strikes out Battey on three pitches and goes to a 2-2 count on Allison before the left fielder takes a hefty cut at a fast ball . . . and misses. Final score: 2-0. Winning pitcher—Koufax (2-1); losing pitcher—Kaat (1-2).

Dodgers win Series, 4 games to 3.

1966

Tough luck and bad breaks kept the Twins in second place after their phenomenal 1965 season. Injuries knocked Allison out for two-thirds of the season, and fat hung on Battey to the extent that Boston's Lu Clinton threw the waddling catcher out, right field to first, after an apparent single. The lineup was juggled. Killebrew began playing third, Mincher played first, Versalles was still at short, though only a shadow of his '65 self, and Bernie Allen was returned to second. Ted Uhlaender filled in for the injured Allison, with Hall and Oliva filling the outfield. The Twins were in second primarily due to the efforts of Cesar "Pepe" Tovar, the Twins' Mr. Versatility. Tovar played second, short and outfield with his "I only geev one hunred an feefte percent" zeal, and was placed in the lead-off spot. The sparkplug's goal was "to play someday in da Worl Serius." Kaat had the season of his career with a 25-13 record. Merritt (13-7), Boswell (12-5), Perry (11-7) and Grant (13-13) rounded out the pitching staff. Pascual (8-6) sat out most of the season with a sore arm. Worthington (6-3 with 16 saves) was all Sam Mele could turn to in the bullpen. Versalles again led the AL in muffs at shortstop, and Battey had to be backed up by Russ Nixon and Jerry Zimmerman. Battey's performance prompted sportscaster Halsey Hall to recall some years later that Battey rounding second base "looked like he was pushing a safe."

1967

If the baseball gods smiled on Minnesota in 1965 they were snarling at the Twins in '67. The Twins went to the wire against Boston and Detroit, with the last two games with the Red Sox deciding their fate. With the Twins jammed with talent, including Dean Chance (acquired by trade) and Rod Carew (rookie of the year), Sam Mele lost his job 50 games into the season with a 25-25 team record. Cal Ermer replaced him and took the team to one of the most fiercely contested pennant races in baseball history. With two games left in Boston, Minnesota needed only one victory to clinch the pennant. On September 30th Boston's Jose Santiago pitched against the Twins' Kaat. Though they loaded the bases in the first, the Twins scored only once, on Oliva's single. Kaat cruised to the third, but with a two-ball no-strike count on Mike Andrews, something went pop in Kaat's arm. Perry replaced Kaat and managed well to the sixth. In the meantime, the Twins, on Rich Reese's pinch hit, upped the score to 2-0. In the Boston sixth, Carew slipped and fell trying to chase down Jerry Adair's pop fly, and it dropped in for a hit, scoring Dalton Jones. Carl Yastrzemski apparently had singled under Killebrew's glove but Carew dove and nabbed the ball. Coming up throwing, Carew had to hold the ball because Perry wasn't covering first, so Jones scored the tying run. In the seventh, George Scott, who hadn't homered in over a month, hit a solo shot off Ron Kline. In the eighth, errors by Kline and Versalles that would have ended the inning left Andrews and Adair on base for Yaz's 44th homer, and the score was 6-2. With Tovar on second, Killebrew launched his 44th homer of the season, but that was it; final score, 6-4. The winner was Santiago, the loser, Ron Kline (the only loss Kline suffered in '67). October 1 pitted Cy Young Award-winner Jim Lonborg against Chance, who had held the Sox hitless in an abbreviated 5-inning affair, and had no-hit the Indians in a 9-inning rout. The Twins took an early 2-0 lead as Oliva doubled home Killebrew, and later Killebrew knocked in Tovar with a single. In the sixth, Boston rallied

The two most popular and effective Twins of the Met Stadium years were Harmon Killebrew and Rod Carew.

with a two out, bases loaded single up the middle by Yaz that scored Adair and Lonborg. An error by Versalles on Ken Harrelson's chopper to short scored Jones. The score was 3-2. Worthington replaced Chance, threw two wild pitches and Yaz scored. A one-hopper off Reggie Smith's bat hit Killebrew in the knee and allowed Jose Tartabull, running for Harrelson, to score from third. The Twins managed a two-out rally in the eighth as Oliva and Killebrew singled and Allison lined a shot off the left field wall, scoring Oliva, but Yaz threw Allison out trying to stretch the hit into a double. The game and season were over. Final score, 5-3; winning pitcher, Lonborg; losing pitcher, Perry. This was the last season for Twins' stalwarts Battey (retired) and Versalles (traded with Grant to the Dodgers for Ron Perranoski, Bob Miller and John Roseboro).

1968

Frustration generated by the end of '67 carried over to '68. This was the year of no-hit baseball. Boston's Yastrzemski captured the AL batting title with the lowest average in modern baseball, .301. Oliva's .289 was third and Uhlaender's .283 was fifth, but the reason the Twins sank to a dismal seventh with a 79-83 record was attributable to the absence of Killebrew, who, in the All-Star game in the Astrodome, stretched for a throw at first and ripped the hamstring tendon in his leg. The Twins were not strong up the middle. Shortstops Ron Clark and Jackie Hernandez were fair fielders and pathetic hitters, and though Roseboro was a good defensive catcher, he was getting old and didn't play every day. His backup was Bruce Look. The outfield was a step quicker with Allison moved in to play first, leaving Tovar, Uhlaender and Oliva in the pasture. Unfortunately, in this year of the pitcher, the only thing Dean Chance improved was his batting average (from .033 to .054) and most of the staff had ERAs over 3 while the league was being sizzled by Tiant (1.60), McDowell (1.81), McNally (1.96) and 30-game-winner McLain (1.96). September 22 was "fun day" at the Met when Griffith put on a P.T. Barnum sideshow, playing Tovar at all nine positions against the Oakland A's. The first man Tovar faced as a pitcher was Bert Campanaris, the only other man in baseball history to play all nine positions in one game. At least the Twins won that one, 2-1. Two major changes affected the Twins: the American League pitching mounds were lowered and the strike zones were narrowed to give hitters a better chance, and Cal Ermer was fired, making way for the managing debut of Billy Martin.

1969

With a temper as red as his champion tomatoes and the blood he spilled on bar room floors, Martin took charge of a team loaded with talent and drove them to the first American League Western Division title. The American League had added the Kansas City Royals (to replace the A's who had left for Oakland) and Seattle Pilots (who appropriately enough played in Sick Stadium—their record was 64-98). The addition of these two teams split the league into two six-team divisions. Pressed by an aggressive Martin style of baseball (Killebrew stole 8 bases!), the Twins easily won the division. This time they did it with the best all-around play that Twins' fans had ever seen. Defensively they were unusually adept, with the addition of Leo Cardenas at short and Rich Reese at first. Killebrew led the league with 49 homers and 149 RBIs, and Carew captured his first silver bat with a .332

average. Season that with Oliva's 24 homers, 101 RBIs and .309 average, Reese's 16 homers, 69 RBIs and .322 average, and Tovar's .273 average with 45 stolen bases,and the Twins were the best team in the American League (on paper). Martin's right cross to Dave Boswell's jaw jolted the young right hander into the best season of his career (20-12) and Jim Perry (20-6) was beginning to show his colors as the Twins stopper. Perranoski was the bullpen (31 saves), but some help came from Worthington (brought out of voluntary retirement to post a 4-1 record with 3 saves) and Bob Miller (5-5 with 3 saves). The first two games of the playoffs against the Orioles were nail biters. Perry, facing Mike Cuellar, pitched to a 3-3 tie in the ninth. In the 12th, Mark Belanger scored on a Paul Blair squeeze play and the Birds won 4-3. The second game was another pitchers' duel, won by Baltimore 1-0 in the 11th. The trip to the East Coast must have unsettled the Twins; they dropped the finale 11-2.

1970

Perhaps it was because Martin punched Twins traveling secretary Howard Fox; perhaps it was the fisticuffs with Boswell outside a Detroit bar; perhaps it was because he publically aired his grievances about the Twins front office in the newspapers; but for one, or all, of the above reasons, Calvin canned Billy and hired Bill "Captain Hook" Rigney. That did not sit well with the fans. "Bring Back Billy" bumper stickers were as prevalent as Humphrey stickers in an election year. A country western song lamented, "Are you leavin' Billy Martin? It's a shame, it's a shame." But Rigney guided the Twins to their second Western Division title in bubble gum and baling wire fashion. Carew's knee was torn up in June and Danny Thompson and Quilici filled in. Uhlaender, Miller and Chance were peddled to Cleveland for Luis Tiant and Stan Williams. Tiant broke his shoulder after a brilliant 7-3 start, so the Twins brought up a 19-year-old, Bert Blyleven, to fill out the weakened starting rotation. Blyleven won his debut, 2-1 over the Senators, and won nine more games that season. The pitching sensation was Cy Young Award-winner Perry (24-12), but whenever he needed help (and considering that Rigney earned his nickname "Captain Hook" by yanking pitchers at the slightest sign of trouble, that was often) Perranoski (34 saves) and Williams (10-1 with 15 saves) constituted the best bullpen in the American League. Cardenas anchored the defense with his brilliant glove, and Tovar became the centerfielder, replacing Uhlaender. Bats boomed with traditional vigor as Oliva and Killebrew both had over 100 RBIs, Carew, Tovar and Oliva all hit .300 or over, and Brant Alyea, the fourth outfielder, cracked 16 homers and 61 RBIs while batting .291. The 1970 playoffs were a rematch of '69 but were hardly similar. The ERA figures for Twins' pitchers looked like prices in Dayton's basement store: Perry 13.50, Perranoski 19.29, Tiant 13.50, Hall and Zepp 6.75, Kaat and Woodson 9.00. Only Blyleven and Williams were unscored upon. The scores were 10-6, 11-3 and 6-1. It was the end of Minnesota's golden years of baseball.

1971

As the Twins began their second decade in Minnesota, they were a team on the decline. For six years they had been one of the powers of the American League. Even in 1968, an off year, most experts realized that the Twins would come back. In 1971 the Twins still had Killebrew (28 homers, 119 RBIs), Tovar (.311, 18 stolen bases, 204 hits) and Carew (.307) but the cold hard truth was that the road back would not be as quick or easy as it was in '68. The strength of the club in the first decade was power, but names like Alyea (2 homers, 15 RBIs, .179 average), Manuel (.125) and Reese (.218) weren't about to make Twins fans forget Allison, Jimmie Hall and Mincher. The cheers for stalwart catchers Battey and Roseboro in the first decade turned to jeers as the fans were forced to endure the likes of Mitterwald, Ratliff, Roof, Dempsey and Tischinski behind the plate in '71. Those names sound like a law firm, but it should have been against the law to play the way those guys did. A pennant-winning pitching staff had disintegrated and the great Tony "O" suffered a serious knee injury late in the season that ended his career in the outfield. In 1971 the Twins drew 945,000 fans, the first time in their 11 seasons in Minnesota that they failed to draw a million. The fans, already mad at Calvin for firing Billy Martin, would not be patient while the Twins took time to rebuild. They were used to a winner, stars and home runs.

1972

Webster's defines "mediocre" as being neither very good nor very bad. The Twins of 1972 were a living example of mediocrity. With a 77-77 third place finish and a team batting average of .244, the Twins' overall performance was certainly mundane, average and, yes, mediocre. The Twins, as a team, were not the best or worst in the league in a single batting, fielding or pitching category. Only one player on the team was a league leader in an individual category. That was Rod Carew, who won the batting title with a .318 average. Even that was somewhat mediocre because Carew became the first American League player in history to win a batting title without hitting a single home run. In 1972, "Captain Hook" Rigney was given the hook by Calvin. He was replaced as Twins manager in June by Frank Quilici. The Twins drew an all-time low 797,901 paying customers. This undoubtedly was due to the Twins' poor showing on the field, but a players' strike at the beginning of the season that wiped out several home dates was also a factor. The fans who did show up at the Met saw a 29-year-old rookie named Bobby Darwin hit a bunch of Killebrew-like homers. He totaled 22 for the year. Killebrew walloped 26, far below his norm, but good enough to lead the team. Rookie third baseman Eric Soderholm was the only other Twin in double figures in homers with 13, but he batted a miserable .188.

Who was Rich Chiles and why is he unique in Twins history?

On July 4, 1977, Chiles, a journeyman outfielder in both the National and American Leagues, became the only person ever to pinch hit for Rod Carew.

Manager Gene Mauch, learning that Carew was injured and unable to swing a bat, inserted Chiles as a pinch hitter against Milwaukee. Chiles responded with a double.

Ironically, in late 1967 the Twins signed veteran outfielder Carroll Hardy who, as a member of the Boston Red Sox, achieved the same kind of notoriety as Chiles when he became the only person every to pinch hit for Ted Williams.

1973

If the fans didn't pay attention to the performance of the 1972 Twins, Calvin Griffith did. He wasted little time churning up the shaky Twins roster. November and March deals sent Wayne Granger, Dave LaRoche, Tovar and Perry (among others) packing, and added names like Larry Hisle, Joe Lis and Joe Decker. Of all the trades Calvin has engineered over the years, the Granger for Hisle deal has to rank as one of the very best. Hisle rapped 15 homers and batted .272 for the Twins in '73 while shoring up an otherwise porous outfield defense. An aging, injured Harmon Killebrew contributed only 5 homers, and the rest of the '73 offense was as harmless. For the first time in the history of the Twins franchise no one hit as many as 20 homers. This was the first year of the designated hitter, a role which prolonged the career of a crippled Oliva who hit .291, slugged 16 homers and knocked in 92 runs (all on one leg!). It was also the year of Eddie Bane, the little lefty hurler who more than repaid his $50,000 bonus by drawing 45,890 fans to the Met on July 4 for his major league debut. Bane didn't win that game or any other in '73, proving that it's tough to win in the majors if you can't throw hard enough to break a pane of glass. The Twins must have found comfort in playing .500 ball in 1972 because this year they managed an encore performance, going 81-81 in a strikeless full season.

1974

Spring of 1974 marked the beginning of the "streaking craze." People of both sexes at college campuses, shopping centers and ball parks were taking off all their clothes and running past crowds of people in broad daylight. The Twins in 1974 were also streakers, but they did it while wearing their uniforms. Early in the season most of their streaks were losing ones. Later, after most rational people in the Midwest had lost all interest, they turned things around. On June 23 the club was 26-39. After that date they were 56-41 to break their .500 habit and post an 82-80 mark, their first winning record since the 1970 divisional championship. Still, 82-80 is hardly championship baseball, and the reason the club failed to do better is obvious: Oliva and Killebrew continued to fade. They each managed but 13 homers, and both were unable to play in the field. Thus, they shared the designated hitter role. Calvin, who wheeled and dealed to get fresh faces in 1973, made only one trade before the '74 season, swapping catchers with the Cubs. The Twins' Mitterwald was sent to the north side of the Windy City for injury-prone Randy Hundley, who played in 32 games and, you guessed it, got injured. Bobby Darwin enjoyed his finest year, slugging 25 homers and driving in 94 runs. One of his homers was a gargantuan shot halfway up in the Met's second deck seats in left field. Only Killebrew had done that before. Carew won his third straight batting crown with an eyepopping .364 mark. The pitching was strikingly unremarkable. Blyleven, Goltz and Decker mirrored the team season record, collectively winning two more games than they lost. The team's best lefty was Vic Albury, whose record was 8-9. No wonder attendance was below a million for the fourth straight year.

1975

This year began with Calvin Griffith publicly stating he was a domed-stadium advocate. A cruel winter which seemed like it would last until Memorial Day undoubtedly prompted Calvin's wish for a dome. Griffith wasn't the only one who was unhappy in 1975. The fans, responding to .500 baseball and miserable weather, stayed away from the Met in record numbers. Several players also were unhappy, having lost at salary arbitration. An unhappy ball club at the start of the season rapidly turned into an unhealthy team as the season progressed. Injuries to such key players as Blyleven, Decker, Hisle, Braun, Brye, Bostock and Soderholm dashed any hopes the Twins had of becoming a contender. However, the announcement that regular Twins shortstop Danny Thompson had leukemia and was being treated by the Mayo Clinic must have made all the injured Twins feel fortunate by comparison. Thompson's disease created chaos at shortstop. Manager Frank Quilici tried to fill the position with Sergio Ferrer, a man whose name sounded like a South American band leader. Unfortunately he fielded like he was one. Later, Luis Gomez, who gave a new meaning to the term banjo hitter (he batted .139), was given a shot at short. Eventually Thompson, his disease in remission, was reinstalled as the regular shortstop. Carew again won the batting crown and upped his homer total from 0 in '72 to 14 in '75. The rest of the Twins also hit well—eight players were in double figures in homers, but the pitching was wanting and the defense pathetic. Since you can't fire all the players, you fire the manager and hope the next year will be better. That's what Calvin did.

1976

Any hopes the Twins had of improving their fortunes in 1976 had to rest with the hiring of new manager Gene Mauch, since the front office did little during the off-season to change the faces which contributed to the 82-80 1975 finish. The Bicentennial version of the Twins offered the fans several unique twists. Second baseman Rod Carew became a first baseman. A 20-year-old graduate of the California League named Harold Delano "Butch" Wynegar became the Twins' starting catcher, and a relief pitcher—Bill "Soupy" Campbell—became the Twins' biggest winner at 17-15. Starter Dave Goltz at 14-14 was the only other pitcher to win in double figures. The Twins began the year as a speedier, younger team with less power than in the past. This was the year the remarkable Tony "O" came to the end of his physical endurance—hobbling off into the sunset with a .211 batting average in only 123 at bats. The Twins batting order no longer was the terror of the American League. Even Bobby Darwin had departed. The Twins played good baseball, but again it was late in the second half of the season, long after most fans stopped paying attention. However, youth, speed and hitting made the prospects for 1977 brighter than they had been in some time.

1977

The subject of the biggest story in baseball in 1977 was Rodney Cline Carew. He received constant attention by the press all over the American League as he nearly became the first hitter since Ted Williams to hit .400. In fact, Carew appeared on the cover of *Sports Illustrated*

Harmon Killebrew's second-deck home run at Met Stadium traveled over 500 feet and was one of only two balls ever hit into the second-deck in left field.

He probably had hair then too! Harmon Killebrew broke into major league baseball as a third baseman for the Washington Senators.

Two of baseball's all-time great hitters, Rod Carew and Ted Williams.

with the Splendid Splinter himself during the season. His picture also appeared on the cover of *Time* next to the headline "Baseball's Best Hitter." He batted .388, easily copping his sixth American League batting title, while rapping out 239 hits, the most in the majors since Heinie Manush had 241 way back in 1928. As remarkable as Rodney's hitting was that year, he was only one of a whole stable of superlative Twins' batsmen. Glenn Adams batted .338, and Lyman Bostock hit .336 with 199 hits, 90 RBIs and 104 runs scored. Hisle batted .302, smacked 28 homers and drove home 119 runs. The Twins as a team had a .282 batting average, the best in the majors, and they scored 867 runs—nearly 5.5 per game. Unfortunately, with the pitching they had and the fielding they lacked, they needed every run they could get—and then some. Tommy Johnson won 16 games in relief and Dave Goltz became the Twins' first 20-game winner since 1973. After that the quality dropped off fast. Six other pitchers on the staff had ERAs of over 5.00. The Twins, while batting or running the bases, were a treat to watch. It was speed and hitting that kept them in contention until Labor Day. Unfortunately, the failure of the pitching staff in September led to the team's downfall. Still, exciting baseball returned to the Met and Twins fans responded by returning to the old ball park to watch the fun. Attendance topped the million mark for the first time since 1970.

1978

If Twins fans could have had three wishes at the beginning of 1978, they undoubtedly would have been (1) Hisle signing with the Twins, (2) Bostock signing with the Twins, and (3) a pennant-winning ball club. Unfortunately the first two wishes did not come true, and that ended any chance of wish No. 3 becoming reality. Bostock and Hisle "played

out their options" and signed with California and Milwaukee, respectively. The addition of "Bombo" Rivera, Hosken Powell and Willie Norwood did not replace the departed free agents at the plate, but the rookies' bats were outstanding compared to the cast iron gloves they brought to the ball park. The ace reliever of 1977, Tommy Johnson, was apparently burned out from overwork the previous year, and in mid-May the Twins hired free agent Mike Marshall to shore up the bullpen. Before Marshall was signed the Twins bullpen comprised Jeff Holly, Gary Serum and Johnny "Ike" Sutton. Therefore, it was not surprising that Marshall made the team. What was surprising was how effective he turned out to be. In 54 games he pitched 99 innings and saved 21 games while posting a 2.36 ERA. Goltz trailed off to 15 wins after his 20-win season, but still led the team in victories. A rookie named Roger Erickson (the pitcher, not the radio announcer) was second in wins with 14. Shortstop Roy Smalley became the Twins' biggest slugger, smashing 19 homers. Only Dan Ford with 11 joined him in double figures in round trippers. The Twins' return to the million attendance mark in 1977 was short-lived as the Twins managed to draw only 787,878 people in '78 while slumping to a 73-89 record.

1979

The Twins had not been in contention for a championship after Labor Day since they won the American League West in 1970. Because of this fact and because of the team's dismal showing in '78, nearly everyone was surprised that the Twins remained in the '79 race until the White Sox eliminated them on September 25. In spite of the Twins' failure to capture the AL West crown, 1,070,521 fans came out to the Met to watch a bona fide contender vie for a post-season berth. The improved showing of the Twins was due at least in part to several new faces on the roster. Jerry Koosman, the Appleton, Minn., native, was obtained from the Mets for a couple of minor league pitchers after "Kooz" announced he'd retire if the Mets failed to trade him to the Twins. The veteran lefty promptly became the ace of the Twins pitching staff, winning 20 games. The Twins also signed "Iron Mike" Marshall to a three-year contract and he earned his $300,000-plus salary, racking up 32 saves. Gone in '79 were superstar Rod Carew and "Disco" Danny Ford, and in their place were young Kenny Landreaux, a fleet outfielder who had broken Reggie Jackson's college records at Arizona State, and Ron Jackson, who proved to be an adept fielder at first base. Jackson anchored a superb infield comprised of Smalley, who set an American League record for shortstops for most assists; Rob Wilfong, outstanding at second base; and a new third baseman, co-Rookie of the Year John Castino, who reminded some fans of Brooks Robinson, the great Baltimore third baseman. Veterans Mike Cubbage at third and Bobby Randall at second gave the Twins depth and prompted manager Mauch to platoon. Smalley led the club in power hitting with 24 homers and 95 runs batted in. Landreaux hit .305 and rapped 15 round-trippers. The pitching was better than it had been in recent years but pickings were thin after "Kooz," Geoff Zahn, Goltz, Marshall and Pete Redfern. The '79 Twins were at their best when their lefthanded batters were in the lineup. Lefty pitchers were poison to the locals since the righthanded batters were especially inept. At season's end, however, more free-agent defections would take their toll and the excitement of '79 would be impossible to match in 1980.

1980

In 1964, Killebrew, Allison and Oliva combined to hit 113 homers. That's 14 more than the entire 1980 team managed. They were godawful. So bad were they that some fans entered the stadium holding their noses in anticipation. Manager Gene Mauch thought they were so rotten that he quit on August 24 after a 3-2 loss to Detroit. As highly touted as Mauch was, he had never won a pennant, and his best finish was second in 1964 when his Phillies blew a 6½ game lead with 12 games left in the season. And *he* was so disgusted with the Twins that he quit. Even the team was disgusted with the team. "We made him quit," Wilfong quipped after Mauch left. Enter John Goryl. He led a fairly successful conclusion of the season, ending 77-84 in third, 19½ games out of the weak AL West. If things weren't bad enough, a team that was critically short of pitching rid itself of its biggest star, Mike Marshall, on June 6. The official reason for Marshall's dismissal was his slow start. The real reason was his active role in a possible players' strike early in the season (which was largely responsible for his slow start). Mauch asked Griffith to cut Marshall from the team (which Calvin did with glee) in spite of the contractual obligation to pay him $300,000-plus for each of two more years. So

forgettable was the play of the '80 Twins that few fans remember that Doug Corbett took over for Marshall with a 1.98 ERA and 23 saves. But pitching wasn't the only problem. The team did not have an outfield capable of catching a fly ball. Dave Edwards had 11 errors, Landreaux bobbled 6, Hosken Powell kicked 9, Rick Sofield had 6 and even Adams, who was supposed to be a designated hitter *only*, "oopsed" 1. The AL West had only two teams above .500 (Kansas City and Oakland), while the AL East had only two teams under .500 (Cleveland and Toronto).

1981

If they were awful in '80, the Twins were worse in '81. The fans were so disgusted with the Twins' 17-39 first half showing that they came to the park wearing paper bags of shame over their heads. This was the year of the players' strike, which was looked upon by Twins' fans as a governor's pardon of a team on death row. Calvin, however, was not so lenient with manager Goryl. The miserable showing was blamed on him, so his brief managerial tenure ended, and Billy Gardner's began. On June 12 the players walked off the job and began a strike that lasted two months. After the strike, the season started over with a second half, with each half-season victor playing off for the divisional title. That decision helped the Twins regain some semblance of self-respect. Nevertheless, it was hard to imagine a major league team that played worse in the "first" season. Glenn Adams was caught off second base in the second game of the season, a victim of the "hidden ball" trick. The team failed to execute simple run-down plays. Pitching was fair, but there was little fielding and no hitting. The second half saw the Twins improve on the field due to the addition of a bunch of kids, all-stars with lower minor league farm clubs. Bloomington native Kent Hrbek, a .380 hitter in the California League, beat the Yankees in his major league debut with a home run. Later Tim Laudner and Gary Gaetti, the Southern League all star catcher and third sacker, respectively, also homered in their first major league games. All three young sluggers were subsequently injured, as was slick-fielding rookie shortstop Lenny Faedo. They were joined on the injured list by Smalley and Castino (bad backs), Wynegar (two injuries), Darrell Jackson (sore shoulder), Erickson (broken thumb), Danny Goodwin (injured hand) and Mickey Hatcher (bone chips). Technically, they were in contention until the last week of the "second" season, but no one really thought the Twins would qualify for post-season play. Even Calvin conceded this fact when, after the last baseball game at the Met was played, he gave away home plate (not the original plate—it was stolen the night before), all the bases and the pitchers' rubber while the Twins were technically still in playoff contention. The Twins finished the 109-game season without a single player reaching double figures in homers. The team batted a miserable .241. No Twins pitcher won as many as 10 games. Despite this fact, the Twins' pitching staff posted a commendable collective 3.78 ERA. Good pitching and the prospect of all that new blood making the team gave fans some hope as the Twins prepared to enter 1982, the year of the Metrodome.

Bill Morlock and Rick Little are the authors of Split Doubleheader, *an unauthorized history of the Minnesota Twins. The 118-page book plus supplement can be obtained by sending a check for $5 to Morick Inc., 6708 Orchard Lane, Minneapolis, MN 55429.*

How the Vikings Came to Be

by JIM KLOBUCHAR

One of the more amiable cavemen of the Minnesota Vikings' middle years was a defensive back named Dale Hackbart, whose place in the pro football archives is secure on two counts:

He performed more out-of-bounds tackles and illegal forearm chops than any player in the Vikings' history, and he was the first man drafted by another Minnesota pro football club that mercifully never played a game.

This second honor may be the more significant, because it reveals the quality of the conniving and disorder that brought Minnesota into the National Football League two decades ago.

The creation of the Vikings represented the only recorded case of an alliance between Minneapolis and St. Paul that was arranged unaided by shotgun-carrying relatives. This alone was enough to make it an object of wonder among sociologists and the natives themselves. It was not an easy union. No unnatural marriages are. Moreover, the formation of the Vikings was less an act of creativity than an act of piracy. As such, it faithfully reflected the rules of war that existed in the early 1960s in the pell-mell battle for a pro football bonanza that hung just over the horizon.

Nobody in those years grasped its immensity. But among those whose nostrils were especially well-tuned to the potential were the Minneapolis triumvirate of H.P. Skoglund, E.W. Boyer and Max Winter. Skoglund was a girthy and forceful insurance tycoon, a man whose influence and crystal-shattering voice from the fjords touched all sectors of the Scandinavian community and reached to the Swedish royalty. Boyer was a smooth-spieling Minneapolis Ford dealer. His silver curls and vaguely Southern burr—an auditory mystery that Boyer never completely explained—made him an absorbing figure to the big league brokers who listened to his annual pitch for a franchise in Minnesota. Winter was a hustler from north Minneapolis who began as a fighter and graduated to boxing promotions, restaurants, theater and auto shows. He functioned on grit, savvy and the survivor's instincts. Eventually he got into the major leagues of sorts as a part-owner of the Minneapolis Lakers, and the experience was heady enough to spur him into partnership with Boyer and Skoglund when pro football began prospecting in Minnesota.

The National Football League itself authorized the first soundings by agreeing to schedule two regular season games of the St. Louis Cardinals in Bloomington's Metropolitan Stadium in 1959. For this the Cardinals received a $240,000 guarantee put up by Twin Cities businessmen eager to dramatize the territory's readiness for pro football. The promoters managed to fill the stadium with tactics considered acceptable in the spirit of the times, including the strongarming of Chamber of Commerce members, gashouse ballyhooing in the newspapers and the shanghaiing of hundreds of freebie recipients off the streets.

On precisely the day of the St. Louis-New York Giants game in November of 1959, the new American Football League opened its organizational meeting at the Nicollet Hotel in Minneapolis.

Boyer, Skoglund and Winter had already been recruited to form a Minneapolis-St. Paul franchise for the new league. They were in that historic number that joined in the Nicollet to pledge its undying devotion to the AFL or, as most of the football public called it, the AF of L.

Among their colleagues were the young Texas millionaires, Lamar Hunt of Dallas and Bud Adams of Houston; ex-Notre Dame coach Frank Leahy, wearing his jumbo bow ties and the colors of Baron Hilton in Los Angeles; the undeflatable former sportscaster Harry Wismer of New York, and a half dozen jock celebs and characters.

On the afternoon of their first meeting, George Halas, the Glowering Bear of the National Football league, sent a telegram to Minneapolis's major league promoters declaring the NFL's intention to offer a franchise to Minnesota at its winter meeting in Miami. The telegram was directed to Charles Johnson, the sports editor of the Minneapolis *Star*. It was released to the press at Met Stadium about the time the public address announcer, Bob Casey, became the first person from Met Stadium to qualify for the Hall of Fame by declaring: "The Giants are penalized 15 yards for having an illegitimate man downfield."

The three Minneapolis entrepreneurs at the Nicollet could not claim to be stunned by the announcement from Halas, who was head of the NFL expansion committee. They practically invited it, despite their nominal allegiance to the new league. The NFL at the time was organizing its strategy to squelch the AFL. An important part of that was to expand into two of the most attractive football territories being sought by the AFL: Dallas and Minneapolis-St. Paul.

Winter, Skoglund and Boyer nonetheless joined the AFL

Norm Van Brocklin inherited the task of molding a group of rookies and castoffs into the original Vikings in 1961.

Midway Stadium offered some unique practice opportunities.

as charter members. A league without a football was better, at least for a couple of months, than a league that still had to poll the members in Miami. As one of its first official acts, therefore, Minneapolis-St. Paul joined in the AFL draft. Hackbart, a bony and strong-armed quarterback from Wisconsin, headed the Minnesota list. The personnel man offered him a contract. But when Hackbart asked about the bonus, the man confided that as a matter of principle, the club was not offering bonuses. Hackbart said he would be the last to want to corrupt somebody's principles. He said adios and headed for Winnipeg.

The triumvirate, however, headed for Miami, where the NFL was ready to vote Minnesota a franchise. Convinced, Winter, Skoglund and Boyer asked the AFL for a release from their franchise charter. Hunt, as the acting chief executive of the league, acceded over the growls of his colleagues. By now the Minneapolis clan had been joined by Bernie Ridder, the publisher of the St. Paul *Dispatch* and *Pioneer Press*, representing St. Paul interests, and by Ole Haugsrud, a gentle gnome of a man from Duluth who was a tobacconist and a promoter. He had no great wealth but he had one indispensable qualification. Years ago he ran an NFL team in Duluth called the Eskimos, whose existence caused no great stir in the march of civilization. The organization melted after a couple of years. But the NFL gave Ole the solemn pledge that if pro football ever came back to Minnesota, Ole would have the right of first refusal.

Ridder knew him well and Ole was adopted as the fifth member of the consortium, holding 10 percent of the stock that was ultimately issued. Ridder spoke for 30 percent and the rest was divided among Winter, Skoglund and Boyer.

The price the NFL imposed, by today's standards, might buy one or two commercials on Sunday afternoon.

"It'll cost you $600,000 to join," the NFL advised the apprentice moguls, "and $400,000 later."

The stock today must be worth 25 times that. A Minneapolis businessman who was offered $10,000 of it in the first month, and turned it down as a marginal investment, says now: "I thought Max was going senile. And now it's 22 years later, and he still does 200 pushups a day and he's worth 25 times what he was. I told him I thought the next great sport in Minnesota was team tennis."

So they hired Bert Rose as general manager, sold 25,000 season tickets the first year, and named Norman (Dutch) Van Brocklin of Philadelphia and Los Angeles as the first coach. The time came for the first joint management-coaching decision.

"Dutch," they said, "we figure to train in Bemidji, 250 miles north of the Twin Cities. There's some objection that this may be too far from the main arteries of publicity."

Van Brocklin examined his first roster of football castaways and orphans.

"With these stiffs," he said, "we don't need publicity. We need concealment."

With these cordial omens was an era begun.

Jim Klobuchar, a columnist for The Minneapolis Star, *has followed the Vikings for two decades as a staff writer for the Associated Press and as a sports writer for both Minneapolis and St. Paul newspapers. He is the author of several books about the Vikings, including* Tarkenton *and* True Hearts and Purple Heads.

Year-by-Year with the Minnesota Vikings

by SCOTT PAPILLON

The Minnesota Vikings, who originated when the National Football League expanded in 1961, have dominated the league's Central Division since the arrival of Head Coach Bud Grant in 1967. The Vikings won the division title 11 times between 1968 and 1980. Here, in capsule form, is a look at the team's 21-year history:

1961 (3-11)

The Minnesota Vikings made an indelible mark on the National Football league by shocking the proud Chicago Bears 37-13 in their very first regular-season game, played before 32,236 fans at Metropolitan Stadium on September 17. After five straight pre-season losses, many Viking backers were expecting the fledgling club to be blown off the field by the Bears. But a youngster named Francis Tarkenton saved the day, leaving the bench to throw four touchdown passes and run for another in relief of George Shaw. Fame was fleeting, however, as the Vikings reverted to expansion-team form and lost their next seven games before beating the Baltimore Colts 28-20. Tarkenton passed for 1,997 yards and 19 touchdowns as a rookie, prompting Coach Norm Van Brocklin to say the third-round pick out of Georgia had "some potential." Many of Tarkenton's passes wound up in the hands of end Jerry Reichow, who caught 50 passes that year for 859 yards and 11 touchdowns. Also making his debut in the starting lineup for the Vikings was a 23-year-old defensive end obtained in a trade with the Cleveland Browns. His name was Jim Marshall.

1962 (2-11-1)

Even though the 1962 won-lost record remains the worst in the history of the franchise, the season was not without merit. The defense allowed 410 points, the most ever by a Vikings team, but Tarkenton kept things lively with his daring scrambles and ability to get a pass off come Hell or Bob Lilly. He fired 22 touchdown passes in 1962, giving him 40 in his first two years, and was especially adept at getting the Vikings points from long range. "We had a 'score from 70-yards-out' offense," Van Brocklin said at the time. Included among the big plays that year was an 89-yard scoring pass from Tarkenton to Charley Ferguson against the Bears, a 74-yarder to Tommy Mason against Philadelphia and a 60-yarder to Ferguson against Pittsburgh. The 89-yard bomb to Ferguson, a hurdler who once competed on the same track team as Wilma Rudolph and Ralph Boston, is still a Vikings record as the longest play from scrimmage. Minnesota's two wins in 1962 came in succession against Los Angeles and Philadelphia and started a string of four straight games in which the Vikings scored 30 or more points. But oh, that defense!

1963 (5-8-1)

The Vikings picked up smooth receiver Paul Flatley in the 1963 draft, but let one big plum get away: defensive lineman Bobby Bell, a University of Minnesota product who signed with the Dallas Texans of the American Football League. Tarkenton's offense generated 22 points per game, however, as the Vikings began showing signs of respectability by winning four of five pre-season games and five more during the regular season. Their biggest accomplishment may have been a late-season 17-17 tie with the Bears. Chicago, which would go on to an 11-1-2 record and the NFL championship, needed a fourth-quarter fumble recovery and an eight-yard TD pass from Bill Wade to Joe Marconi to escape with the tie. Tommy Mason, the guitar-strumming halfback, finished with 763 yards rushing, fifth in the league, to establish himself as one of the premier players in the NFL.

1964 (8-5-1)

With a Pro Bowl backfield of Tarkenton, Mason and Bill Brown, the Vikings posted their best record ever, 8-5-1, in 1964 and people began to take them seriously for the first time. The young club's offense outscored the defense for the first time also, 355-296, thanks in part to a rookie end named Carl Eller. Eller and his linemate, Jim Marshall, also combined on one of the most celebrated and best-remembered plays in Vikings history. On October 25, at

First Viking Lineup
(vs. Chicago Bears, Sept 14, 1961)

	OFFENSE		DEFENSE
E	Dave Middleton	E	Jim Marshall
E	Dick Haley	E	Don Joyce
T	Grady Alderman	T	Jim Prestel
T	Frank Youso	T	Bill Bishop
G	Gary Huth	LB	Karl Rubke
G	Mike Rabold	LB	Rip Hawkins
C	Bill Lapham	LB	Clancy Osborne
QB	George Shaw	CB	Dick Pesonen
HB	Hugh McElhenny	CB	Jack Morris
FB	Mel Triplett	S	Charlie Sumner
TE	Bob Schnelker	S	Rich Mostardi

Kezar Stadium in San Francisco, Eller caused a fumble by quarterback Billy Kilmer. Marshall, always an adventurous sort, scooped up the ball and ran 66 yards—the wrong way—for a 49er safety. Tarkenton had another banner year, passing for 22 touchdowns and being named MVP in the Pro Bowl. Bill Brown became the workhorse in the backfield, rushing for 866 yards and seven touchdowns and catching 48 passes for nine TDs.

1965 (7-7)

Everyone expected great things of the Vikings in 1965, but the team had to settle for a disappointing 7-7 record. The season became memorable, though, with Van Brocklin's one-day resignation following a 41-21 loss to Baltimore in a game which saw Gary Cuozzo replace the legendary Johnny Unitas and throw five touchdown passes. That game also marked the first of four straight losses by the Vikings, but they managed to re-group long enough to win the final two games of the year for a respectable .500 ledger. Minnesota made a key addition with the drafting of running back Dave Osborn on the 13th round, not realizing at the time that the Cando, N.D., runner would eventually establish himself as the epitome of what Viking football would become a few years later. The Vikings also made Jack Snow their No. 1 pick, but he was shipped to Los Angeles. Lance Rentzel, the No. 2 choice, didn't get much playing time in the two years he spent with the Vikings. But he did etch his name into the record books by returning a kickoff 101 yards for a touchdown against the Baltimore Colts.

1966 (4-9-1)

The Vikings entered the second half of their first decade with high hopes, but the 1966 season turned out to be one of the low-water marks in the team's history. Van Brocklin became disenchanted with Tarkenton's impromptu style of quarterbacking and Tarkenton became disenchanted with Van Brocklin as well. More than the 4-9-1 record, it was the breakdown in communication between the two which led to the departure of both. For Tarkenton, the ultimate embarrassment came in the final home game of the year against Atlanta. Tarkenton, a Georgia native, was benched by Van Brocklin in favor of young Bob Berry, even though the game was being televised back to Tarkenton's home state. The Falcons, in their first season, intercepted five passes, scored 20 points in the second quarter and held on for a 20-13 victory while Tarkenton steamed on the bench. The Vikings lost five of their final six games that year and by February of 1967 it was clear that moves would have to be made. Those moves came quickly. In February Van Brocklin resigned, this time for good. Tarkenton, who had submitted a letter saying he no longer wanted to be associated with the Vikings, was traded to the New York Giants in March.

1967 (3-8-3)

The 1967 season marked the end of the Norm Van Brocklin-Fran Tarkenton era and the beginning of the Bud Grant-who's-at-quarterback era. Grant, a disciplinarian, journeyed south from Winnipeg, where he had been a successful Canadian Football League coach for many years. Waiting for him in Minnesota was a merry band of warriors schooled in the swashbuckling style of Van Brocklin and Tarkenton. Grant decided the easiest way for him to get their undivided attention was to put them at attention—literally—during the playing of the national anthem before each game. The acceptance may have been slow at first, but the wait for results would be brief...only two years until the Vikings' first division championship. The nucleus Grant inherited from Van Brocklin wasn't all that bad. Players such as Mick Tingelhoff, Jim Marshall, Bill Brown and Dave Osborn proved to be just the type of athletes Grant wanted: tough, hardworking and dedicated. Then there was the satchelful of high-draft picks because of the Tarkenton and Tommy Mason trades. With those trades came three No. 1 picks: Clint Jones, Gene Washington and Alan Page, plus No. 2 choice Bobby Grim. It was the start of a long success story.

1968 (8-6)

The 1968 Vikings, now adapting quickly to Grant's conservative style of coaching, rode a roller coaster to their first divisional title. After a 3-1 start, Minnesota lost three in a row, won three straight, dropped two more and then finally won the last two games of the season. Against Baltimore in the playoffs, quarterback Joe Kapp threw a pair of touchdown passes, but Earl Morrall, the top-ranked quarterback in the NFL, also threw a pair while Mike Curtis returned a fumble 60 yards for a score to highlight a 24-14 win for the Colts. In the Runnerup Bowl against Dallas, young Bobby Bryant, in his first season, returned a punt 81 yards for a touchdown. Fred Cox kicked two field goals as the Vikings built a 13-0 lead before Don Meredith and Craig Morton each tossed touchdown passes to rally the Cowboys to a 17-13 triumph. This year also saw the addition of offensive tackle Ron Yary, the NFL's No. 1 draft pick, as completion of the previous year's Tarkenton trade.

1969 (12-2)

In 1969, the Vikings nearly reached the zenith of professional football by winning the NFL championship and earning a berth in the Super Bowl. Although a 23-7 Super Bowl loss to the Kansas City Chiefs stunned them and most of the NFL, it did not diminish the accomplishments of a brilliant season. After losing the opening game of the season, 24-23 to Tarkenton and the New York Giants, the Vikings reeled off 12 consecutive victories, then a league record. Highlighting the surge was a 52-14 triumph over Baltimore in the second week. Quarterback Joe Kapp, who would later leave the team and eventually be forced out of pro football, fired seven touchdown passes in that game to tie the NFL record. Minnesota ran roughshod over its opponents that season, outscoring them 379-133 and racing past Los Angeles and Cleveland in the playoffs. The win over the Rams, on Dec. 27 at a chilly Met Stadium, ranks as one of the most exciting Vikings games ever, with Minnesota overcoming a 10-point deficit to win 23-20, capped by Eller's sack of quarterback Roman Gabriel in the end zone for a fourth-quarter safety.

1970 (12-2)

The Vikings opened the 1970 season by extracting a measure of revenge against the Kansas City Chiefs, pummeling them 27-10 at the Met. The Minnesota defense held the defending Super Bowl champions to just eight first downs and 121 net yards. This was a season of considerable accomplishment turned sour by a loss to San Francisco in the first round of the playoffs. The Vikings won nine of their first 10 games and coasted to a third division title on the strength of an awesome defense which allowed just 143 points. Among that season's many highlights was a crushing 54-13 win over the Dallas

Met Stadium's cold weather took its playoff toll on the Cleveland Browns.

Cowboys, who would eventually advance to Super Bowl V. Sparking the victory over Dallas were Fred Cox, who booted four field goals, and defensive back Ed Sharockman, who returned a blocked punt 23 yards for a touchdown and an interception 34 yards for another score. In the playoffs, Minnesota was knocked off 17-14 by the 49ers. The Vikings scored in the first quarter, on Paul Krause's 22-yard fumble return, and on the last play from scrimmage, a 24-yard pass from Gary Cuozzo to Gene Washington with one second left in the game.

1971 (11-3)

This season is remembered for two reasons: It was the year defensive tackle Alan Page became the first defensive player in the history of the NFL to win the Most Valuable Player award; and it was also the season the Vikings played musical chairs with their quarterbacks. Page, the All American from Notre Dame, became the first rookie to start for Grant. His presence in the middle of the Vikings' defensive line gave ends Carl Eller and Jim Marshall more freedom to rush the quarterback, and by 1971 the feats of this line, dubbed the Purple People Eaters, were legendary. In 1971, Gary Cuozzo started eight games at quarterback, Norm Snead two and young Bobby Lee five, including the Vikings' 20-12 playoff loss to Dallas. Because the defense was so strong, allowing only 139 points in 14 games, Grant could afford to gamble and experiment with his quarterbacks. Cuozzo got the Vikings a key 16-13 victory over Detroit in the first game of the season, but when the Vikings lost 20-17 the next week, he

was benched in favor of Snead. Snead led the Vikings to back-to-back shutouts—19-0 over Buffalo and 13-0 over Philadelphia—but Cuozzo was inserted for the next five games. Bobby Lee worked his way into the starting lineup for four of the last five games, but when he struggled against the Cowboys in the playoffs, he was lifted in favor of Cuozzo. It would be the last game in which the Vikings had an unresolved quarterback situation.

1972 (7-7)

The 1972 Vikings will no doubt go down in history as one of the most enigmatic of all Bud Grant teams. Certainly, there were key injuries throughout the season, but defensive lapses and crucial missed kicks were probably more to blame for a third-place finish. Tarkenton, re-acquired from the Giants in a trade which sent Snead, two other players and two draft picks to New York, passed for more than 2,600 yards and threw 18 touchdowns, but even his performance and the acquisition of fleet receiver John Gilliam were not enough. Standing 2-4 after six games, the Vikings won four straight games before losing to Pittsburgh 23-10. Minnesota then defeated Chicago for a 7-5 record going into a crucial game with the Green Bay Packers. Green Bay won the game 23-7, with Minnesota's only score coming on a rare reverse to tight end Stu Voigt. The Vikings' offense managed only 141 yards of total offense that game, 54 rushing, and it was obvious that the team needed a running threat to go with Tarkenton's passing. The Vikings obtained that threat the following spring when they drafted Chuck Foreman.

1973 (12-2)

Minnesota rebounded from its disappointing 1972 season by posting a 12-2 mark in 1973 and advancing to the Super Bowl for the second time. Led by Tarkenton and the young rookie Foreman, the Vikings won nine straight games at the start of the season. Foreman was named NFL Rookie of the Year by *Pro Football Weekly* and NFL Offensive Rookie of the Year by the Associated Press for his team-high 801 yards rushing and 37 pass receptions. Tarkenton, now thoroughly familiar with Bud Grant's system, hooked up 42 times with Gilliam for eight touchdowns, plus a 54-yard bomb against Dallas in the NFC championship game which stunned the Cowboys on their own turf. In Super Bowl VIII, however, the Vikings were simply run off the field by the Miami Dolphins. Larry Csonka set a Super Bowl record by rushing for 145 yards, and quarterback Bob Griese had to throw only seven passes, completing six. Tarkenton, meanwhile, had to put the ball in the air 28 times. He completed 18 of them, a Super Bowl record since tied by Ron Jaworski.

1974 (10-4)

Another successful season, 1974 saw the addition of linebackers Fred McNeill and Matt Blair, players who would become integral parts of the club into the 1980s. Minnesota again started strong, winning seven of its first nine games. The Vikings also won their final three games and then dispatched St. Louis and stubborn Los Angeles to capture a third Super Bowl berth. Super Bowl IX was again unkind to the Vikings, however, who were totally stymied by the swarming defense of the Pittsburgh Steelers. The final score was 16-6. Minnesota managed just nine first downs and only 17 yards rushing, still a Super Bowl low. The season was a statistical success, though. Tarkenton moved into second place in two all-time passing categories—pass attempts and completions.

Foreman shunned the sophomore jinx by rushing for 777 yards, catching 53 passes and leading the NFL with 15 touchdowns.

1975 (12-2)

What loomed as possibly the best Vikings season ever came to an abrupt halt in the very first playoff game when Roger Staubach of the Dallas Cowboys lofted a 50-yard touchdown pass to Drew Pearson in the final moments of the game to derail Minnesota 17-14. The controversial "Hail Mary" pass is still talked about by Vikings fans, many of whom felt that Pearson should have been penalized for offensive interference against cornerback Nate Wright. The bitter, season-ending loss couldn't diminish the achievements of several individuals. Tarkenton fired 25 touchdown passes, a club record, and also set league records for pass attempts in a career and most completions in a career. Foreman blossomed into one of the NFL's premier all-purpose running backs, gaining 1,070 yards rushing, catching a league-high 73 passes and scoring 22 touchdowns, just one short of the NFL record set by O.J. Simpson the same year. Safety Paul Krause picked off 10 passes, pushing his career interception total to 74, only five behind the all-time record set by Emlen Tunnell.

1976 (11-2-1)

Another superlative season ended in disappointment as the Vikings rolled to an 11-2-1 regular season record, breezed past Washington and Los Angeles in the playoffs and roared into Super Bowl XI against Oakland. Bud Grant said he felt his team was as prepared for the Raiders as they could be for any game, but it was little consolation in light of a 32-14 loss. Sparked by Clarence Davis, who gained 137 yards rushing, and Ken Stabler, who completed 12 of 19 passes for 180 yards, Oakland built a 19-0 lead before Tarkenton threw an 8-yard scoring pass to rookie Sammy White. Minnesota's other touchdown came on a 13-yard pass from Bobby Lee to Stu Voigt. Tarkenton added to his personal list of accomplishments during the year, passing for 2,961 yards to surpass Unitas as the all-time leader in virtually every major passing category. Foreman had his best rushing year with 1,155 yards, including a 200-yard game against Philadelphia.

1977 (9-5)

Some said the Vikings were on the road to yet another Super Bowl appearance when the unthinkable happened on Sunday, November 13, at Met Stadium. En route to what turned out to be an easy 42-10 victory over the Cincinnati Bengals, a young, 270-pound defensive lineman named Gary Burley broke through the Vikings' offensive line and sacked Tarkenton. In the process, Burley fell on Tarkenton and broke the scrambler's leg. As Tarkenton was wheeled off the field, many of the fans were thinking "There go the playoffs," but backups Bobby Lee and rookie Tommy Kramer took care of that. The 1977 season will be remembered not only as the year in which Tarkenton was finally sidelined by injury after 17 seasons, but also as the year of Kramer's miracle performance against San Francisco. The 49ers appeared to have the Vikings all but eliminated from the playoffs with a 24-7 lead through three quarters, but Kramer came off the bench in relief of Lee and threw three touchdown passes in the final quarter for a 28-27 victory. Once a playoff berth was secured, Grant went back to Lee to direct the Vikings in the first game against the Rams. Lee, the steady veteran who had played in Tarkenton's shadow for many years, responded with a 14-7 win over the Rams in what has now become known as the "Mud Bowl" in the L.A.

The Purple People Eaters, from left: Jim Marshall, Alan Page, Carl Eller and Gary Larson.

Fran Tarkenton and Coach Bud Grant wait for the defense to get the ball back into Tarkenton's hands.

Coliseum. In the next game, Fred Cox kicked two field goals, Minnesota's only scoring, in a 23-6 loss to Dallas. It marked the last game for Cox, who retired to his chiropractic business with 1,365 career points.

1978 (8-5-1)

Fran Tarkenton returned for one final season in 1978 and got the Vikings into another playoff, although they had to back in by winning just one of their five last games. The 1978 season is notable for two reasons: As Tarkenton's final year, it marked the end of an era and the beginning of a rebuilding process which continued into the early 1980s. The other major occurrence happened during a Monday night game between the Vikings and Bears in Chicago. The Vikings won the game 24-20, but running back Chuck Foreman, the hub of the Minnesota offense for five years, suffered a knee injury which led to the premature end of a dazzling career. Foreman, the greatest runner in Vikings history, gained just 749 yards in 1978, a career low, and would be relegated to backup duty behind Ted Brown in 1979 before finally being sent to New England in 1980. Although the Vikings were dismantled 34-10 in the first round of the playoffs by Los Angeles, the season was not without highlights. Minnesota defeated both of the 1978 Super Bowl teams: Denver 12-9 in overtime, and Dallas 21-10. Both came in nationally-televised contests. Also, Tarkenton added to his many career records and finished with the following NFL records, among others: most passing attempts (6,467), most completions (3,686), most passing yards (47,003) and most touchdown passes (342).

1979 (7-9)

The 1979 season, Minnesota's first without Tarkenton since he rejoined the team in 1972, was a curious one. The Vikings stood 4-4 at the halfway point, but then lost three straight games to fall out of contention in the NFC Central Division, a division they dominated for a decade. The Vikings seemed to play their best against the better teams, however. Kramer, in his first full year as the club's regular quarterback, tossed three touchdown passes against Tampa Bay as Minnesota delayed the Buccaneers' division championship hopes with a 23-22 victory. The

following week, Kramer passed for 297 yards and three more TDs as the Vikings put a scare into Los Angeles before the Rams took a 27-21 overtime victory. Two weeks later, on the final day of the season, Kramer put the ball in the air 61 times and passed for 308 yards in a 27-23 loss to powerful New England. The Vikings' No. 1 draft pick, Ted Brown, also showed signs of becoming the great runner the Vikings hoped he would be.

1980 (9-7)

The 1980 season will be remembered as the year of the Miracle—Tommy Kramer's 46-yard pass to Ahmad Rashad on the last play of the game which clinched the Vikings' 11th division championship. The victory was as impressive in its development as it was in its conclusion. Minnesota trailed 23-9 in the fourth quarter, but scored 19 points in the final seven minutes, capped by Rashad's backpedaling catch, to win 28-23. Bobby Bryant, who would retire before the 1981 season began, set up a touchdown with an interception, the 51st of his career. On the Vikings' final drive, they went 80 yards with no time outs, using a flea-flicker pass from Kramer to Joe Senser, who then lateralled the ball to Ted Brown. Brown raced to the sidelines at the Cleveland 46 with five seconds to play. The 1980 campaign was also remembered as a tale of two seasons. The Vikings were 3-5 in the first half, but 6-2 in the second. Coach Bud Grant was quick to point out the correlation between the Vikings' second-half surge and their move into a new practice facility in Eden Prairie that fall.

1981 (7-9)

What was expected to be a promising 1981 season—the Vikings' final one in Metropolitan Stadium—ended with the disappointment of a five-game losing streak and the callous ravaging of the Met following the final game against Kansas City.

The Vikings rebounded from an 0-2 start to win five consecutive games, as quarterback Tommy Kramer engineered sterling back-to-back victories over San Diego and Philadelphia. Minnesota, in fact, held a seemingly comfortable two-game lead in the NFC Central Division with a 7-4 record, but blew a 21-7 lead against Atlanta on a Monday night game, which proved to be the start of a five-game slide.

Kramer looked like an all-pro quarterback during the winning streak. He finished the year with 26 touchdown passes, fourth highest in the league, and 3,912 yards, second only to Dan Fouts. But his play suffered greatly in the last month, when most of his NFC-high 24 interceptions occurred.

Kramer wasn't the only Viking player to experience the season-ending slump. Running back Ted Brown, who was on his way toward a 2,000-yard season in rushing and receiving, suddenly found the yardage hard to come by as opposing defenses found the cure for Minnesota's short passing game.

The Vikings' defense, which had given up just 10 points in victories over division-winner Tampa Bay and New Orleans, was ripped for 121 points in the next four games, including an embarrassing 45-7 rout by the Detroit Lions in the Silverdome, the second-worst defeat in Minnesota history.

Scott Papillon, a former sports editor of the Associated Press bureau in Minneapolis, now writes for the Minneapolis Star.

Jim Marshall (70) and Alan Page stopped numerous Chicago Bears as part of the Vikings' dominating Purple People Eater defense.

Memorable Viking Moments, clockwise from right: All-Pro Defensive Tackle Alan Page; a typical crowd braced for a sub-freezing early December game; fiery quarterback Joe Kapp; running back Ed Marinaro before he became a cop on "Hill Street Blues;" running back Chuck Foreman, who holds most Viking rushing records.

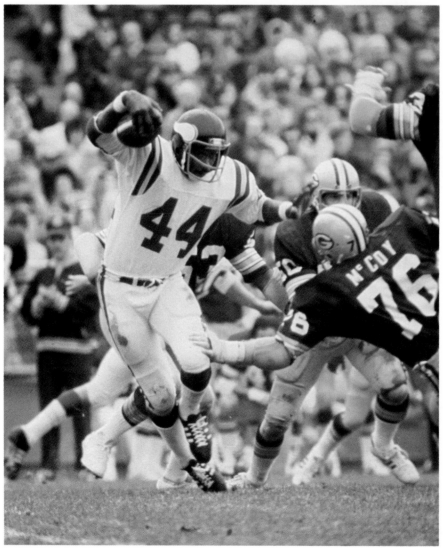

Fran Tarkenton set nearly every National Football League passing record and brought smiles to the faces of thousands of Viking fans and at least one head coach.

Minnesota Vikings: Statistics

SUPER BOWLS

The Minnesota Vikings played in four Super Bowls between 1969 and 1976, losing each time. Here are the results of those games:

1969—Kansas City 23, Minnesota 7 (Super Bowl IV, New Orleans)
1973—Miami 24, Minnesota 7 (Super Bowl VIII, Houston)
1974—Pittsburgh 16, Minnesota 6 (Super Bowl IX, New Orleans)
1976—Oakland 32, Minnesota 14 (Super Bowl XI, Pasadena)

VIKING PRO BOWL PLAYERS

The year designated is the year in which the game was played. Selection is based upon the players' performances in the preceding calendar year.

1962—Hugh McElhenny, halfback; Jerry Reichow, end.
1963—Tommy Mason, halfback.
1964—Mason, halfback; Grady Alderman, tackle; Rip Hawkins, linebacker.
1965—Mason, halfback; Alderman, tackle; Mick Tingelhoff, center; Fran Tarkenton, quarterback; Bill Brown, fullback.
1966—Alderman, tackle; Brown, fullback; Tarkenton, quarterback; Tingelhoff, center.
1967—Paul Flatley, end; Alderman, tackle; Milt Sunde, guard; Tingelhoff, center.
1968—Tingelhoff, center; Alderman, tackle; Brown, fullback.
1969—Tingelhoff, center; Brown, fullback; Carl Eller, defensive end; Jim Marshall, defensive end; Alan Page, defensive tackle.
1970—Eller, defensive end; Joe Kapp, quarterback; Paul Krause, safety; Gary Larsen, defensive tackle; Marshall, defensive end; Page, defensive tackle; Gene Washington, wide receiver; Tingelhoff, center.
1971—Fred Cox, kicker; Eller, defensive end; Karl Kassulke, safety; Larsen, defensive tackle; Dave Osborn, halfback; Page, defensive tackle; Washington, wide receiver.
1972—Eller, defensive end; Page, defensive tackle; Krause, safety; Ron Yary, tackle; Bob Grim, wide receiver.
1973—John Gilliam, wide receiver; Krause, safety; Page, defensive tackle; Yary, tackle.
1974—Chuck Foreman, running back; Gilliam, wide receiver; Krause, safety; Page, defensive tackle; Jeff Siemon, linebacker; Yary, tackle; Eller, defensive end.
1975—Eller, defensive end; Foreman, running back; Gilliam, wide receiver; Krause, safety; Page, defensive tackle; Tarkenton, quarterback; Yary, tackle.
1976—Bobby Bryant, corner back; Foreman, running back; Gilliam, wide receiver; Krause, safety; Page, defensive tackle; Siemon, linebacker; Tarkenton, quarterback; Ed White, guard; Yary, tackle.
1977—Siemon, linebacker; White, guard; Yary, tackle; Sammy White, wide receiver; Foreman, running back; Tarkenton, quarterback; Page, defensive tackle.
1978—Matt Blair, linebacker; Foreman, running back; Siemon, linebacker; E. White, guard; S. White, wide receiver; Yary, tackle.
1979—Blair, linebacker; Ahmad Rashad, wide receiver.
1980—Blair, linebacker; Rashad, wide receiver.
1981—Blair, linebacker; Rashad, wide receiver.
1982—Blair, linebacker; Rashad, wide receiver; Joe Senser, tight end.

Scoring
Viking Career
1,365, Fred Cox
  456, Bill Brown
  450, Chuck Foreman

Season
132, Chuck Foreman, 1975

Game
24, Chuck Foreman vs Buf., 20 Dec 75
24, Ahmad Rashad vs SF., 2 Sept. 79

Most Consecutive Games
151, Fred Cox (NFL record)

Touchdowns
Viking Career
76, Bill Brown
75, Chuck Foreman

Season
22, Chuck Foreman, 1975

Game
4, Chuck Foreman vs Buf., 20 Dec 75
4, Ahmad Rashad vs SF., 2 Sept 79

Field Goals
Viking Career
282, Fred Cox

Season
30, Fred Cox, 1970

Game
5, Fred Cox vs Chi., 23 Sept 73

Most Consecutive Games
31, Fred Cox (5 games 1968 to 12 games 1970, NFL record)

Longest
53, Fred Cox vs GB., 5 Dec 65

Conversions
Viking Career
519, Fred Cox

Season
44, Fred Cox, 1965

Game
7, Fred Cox vs Balt., 28 Sept 69 and Pitt., 3 Nov 69

Rushing Yards
Viking Career
5,879, Chuck Foreman
5,757, Bill Brown

Season
1,155, Chuck Foreman, 1976 (278 attempts)

Game
200, Chuck Foreman vs Phil., 24 Oct 76 (28 attempts)
155, Dave Osborn vs GB., 3 Dec 67
155, Clinton Jones vs Atl., 28 Nov 71

Longest
80, Clinton Jones vs Chi., 2 Nov 69 (touchdown)
73, Dave Osborn vs SF., 17 Sept 67 (touchdown)

Rushing Attempts
Viking Career
1,786, Bill Brown (Lifetime, 1,808)

Season
280, Chuck Foreman, 1975

Game
33, Chuck Foreman vs SD., 23 Nov 75 (127 yds) and Det., 17 Dec 77 (156 yds)

Touchdowns Rushing
Viking Career
52, Bill Brown
52, Chuck Foreman

Season
13, Chuck Foreman, 1975 and 1976

Game
3, Tommy Mason vs SF., 24 Oct 65
3, Clinton Jones vs Det., 15 Nov 70
3, Chuck Foreman vs GB., 15 Sept 74
3, Chuck Foreman vs SD., 23 Nov 75

Longest
80, Clinton Jones vs Chi., 2 Nov 69
73, Dave Osborn vs SF., 17 Sept 67

100 Yard Rushing Games
Viking Career
17, Chuck Foreman

Season
5, Chuck Foreman, 1975

Passing Yards
Viking Career
33,098, Francis Tarkenton (Lifetime, 47,003, NFL record)

Season
3,912, Tommy Kramer, 1981
3,582, Tommy Kramer, 1980
3,468, Francis Tarkenton, 1978

Game
456, Tommy Kramer vs Clev., 14 Dec 80
449, Joe Kapp vs Balt., 28 Sept 69
444, Tommy Kramer vs SD., Oct. 11 81

Most Consecutive Seasons 1,000-plus
18, Fran Tarkenton (NFL record)

Most Consecutive Seasons 2,000-plus
15, Fran Tarkenton (NFL record)

Longest
89, Francis Tarkenton to Charley Ferguson vs Chi., 11 Nov 62
85, Joe Kapp to Gene Washington vs StL., 8 Oct 67

Pass Attempts
Viking Career
4,569, Francis Tarkenton (Lifetime, 6,469, NFL record)

Season
593, Tommy Kramer, 1981
572, Francis Tarkenton, 1978

Game
62, Steve Dils vs Tampa Bay, 5 Sept 81
61, Tommy Kramer vs NE., 16 Dec 79
56, Francis Tarkenton vs Phil., 3 Dec 78

Pass Completions
Viking Career
2,635, Francis Tarkenton (Lifetime, 3,686, NFL record)

Season
345, Francis Tarkenton, 1978

Game
38, Tommy Kramer vs Green Bay, 29 Nov 81
38, Tommy Kramer vs Clev., 14 Dec 80
35, Tommy Kramer vs NE., 16 Dec 79

Most Consecutive Completions
16, Tommy Kramer vs GB., 11 Nov 79
13, Francis Tarkenton vs LA., 3 Dec 61

Pass Completion Percentage
Viking Career
57.6, Francis Tarkenton (Lifetime, 57.0)

Season
64.2, Francis Tarkenton, 1975

Game
84.0, Francis Tarkenton vs Sea., 14 Nov 76 (26 of 31; 20-pass min.)

Pass Interception Percentage (low)
Viking Career
4.2, Francis Tarkenton

Season
1.9, Francis Tarkenton, 1976

Most Consecutive Attempts Without Interception
155, Francis Tarkenton (7 Nov to 5 Dec 77)

Touchdowns Passing
Viking Career
239, Francis Tarkenton (Lifetime, 342, NFL record)

Season
26, Tommy Kramer, 1981
25, Francis Tarkenton, 1975 and 1978

Game
7, Joe Kapp vs Balt., 28 Sept 69 (ties NFL record)

Most Consecutive Games
13, Francis Tarkenton (1 Game 1974, 12 Games 1975)

Longest
89, Francis Tarkenton to Charley Ferguson vs Chi., 11 Nov 62
85, Joe Kapp to Gene Washington vs StL., 8 Oct 67

Pass Receiving Yards
Viking Career
5.256, Ahmad Rashad (Lifetime, 6,598)
3,297, John Gilliam

Season
1,156, Ahmad Rashad, 1979 (80 rec.)
1,095, Ahmad Rashad, 1980 (69 rec.)
1,035, John Gilliam, 1972 (47 rec.)

Game
210, Sammy White vs Det., 7 Nov 76
(7 rec.)

Longest
89, Charley Ferguson from Francis
Tarkenton vs Chi., 11 Nov 62
85, Gene Washington from Joe Kapp vs
StL., 8 Oct 67

Pass Receptions
Viking Career
377, Ahmad Rashad (Lifetime, 472)
336, Chuck Foreman

Season
88, Rickey Young, 1978

Game
15, Rickey Young vs NE., 16 Dec 79
12, Rickey Young vs NO., 3 Sept 78

Most by Wide Receiver
80, Ahmad Rashad, 1979

Most by Rookie
51, Paul Flatley, 1963
51, Sammy White, 1976

Touchdowns Receiving
Viking Career
35, Sammy White

Season
11, Jerry Reichow, 1961
10, Sammy White, 1976

Game
4, Ahmad Rashad vs SF., 2 Sept 79

Most Consecutive Games
4, Sammy White (1977 and 1978)

Most Games One Season
8, Jerry Reichow, 1961
8, Bill Brown, 1964
8, Sammy White, 1977

Longest
89, Charley Ferguson from Francis
Tarkenton vs Chi., 11 Nov 62
85, Gene Washington from Joe Kapp vs
StL., 8 Oct 67

Combined Net Yards
(Rushing, Receiving, Returns)
Viking Career
9,097, Bill Brown (5,716 rushing; 3,136
receiving; 245 returns. Lifetime,
9,339; 5,838 rushing; 3,183 receiving;
318 returns)
8,970, Chuck Foreman (5,879 rushing,
3,057 receiving, 34 returns)

Season
1,761, Chuck Foreman, 1975 (1,070
rushing, 691 receiving)

Pass Interceptions
Viking Career
53, Paul Krause (Lifetime, 81, NFL
record)
51, Bobby Bryant

Season
10, Paul Krause, 1975

Game
3, Roy Winston vs SF., 25 Oct 64
3, Earsell Mackbee vs Det., 26 Oct 69

3, Bobby Bryant vs Clev., 9 Nov 69
3, Ed Sharockman vs Bos., 13 Dec 70
3, Bobby Bryant vs GB., 8 Dec 73
3, John Turner vs Chi., 12 Oct 80

Blocked Kicks
Viking Career
18, Matt Blair
15, Alan Page

Season
5, Alan Page, 1976 (3 PAT, 2 FG)
5, Matt Blair, 1979 (5 PAT)

Punting
Season Attempts
90, Greg Coleman, 1979 (39.5)

Season Average
46.4, Bobby Walden, 1964 (72 punts)

Most Game Attempts
10, Greg Coleman vs Buf., 9 Dec 79
(35.7)

Fewest Game Attempts
0, Neil Clabo vs Det., 7 Nov 76
0, Greg Coleman vs Green Bay, 27
Sept 81

Longest Return
Punt
98, Charlie West vs Wash., 3 Nov 68
(touchdown)
81, Hugh McElhenny vs Chi., 17 Dec 61
(touchdown)
81, Bob Grim vs NY., 5 Nov 67

Kickoff
101, Lance Rentzel vs Balt.,
14 Nov 65 (touchdown)
99, Eddie Payton vs Oakland,
14 Sept 81
96, Clinton Jones vs NY., 5 Nov 67
(touchdown)

Interception
89, Charlie West vs Chi., 19 Dec 71
81, Paul Krause vs SD., 23 Nov 75

Fumble
88, Ed Sharockman vs Det., 9 Dec 61
(touchdown)

Fumbles Recovered
Viking Career
29, Jim Marshall (NFL record)

Season
9, Don Hultz, 1963 (NFL record)

Games Played
Most Consecutive League Games
282, Jim Marshall (NFL record)
240, Mick Tingelhoff

*Most Consecutive League Games—One
Club*
270, Jim Marshall (NFL record)

Most Victories
Viking Career
138, Bud Grant

MINNESOTA VIKINGS
FIRST ROUND DRAFT CHOICES

1961 - Tommy Mason, RB, Tulane
1962 - Traded to New York (for George Shaw)
1963 - Jim Dunaway, DT, Mississippi State
1964 - Carl Eller, DE, Minnesota
1965 - Jack Snow, WR, Notre Dame
1966 - Jerry Shay, DT, Purdue
1967 a- Clinton Jones, RB, Michigan State (choice from N.Y. Giants)
       b- Gene Washington, WR, Michigan State
       c- Alan Page, DT, Notre Dame (choice from Los Angeles)
1968 a- Ron Yary, T, Southern California (choice from N.Y. Giants)
       b- Traded to New Orleans (for Gary Cuozzo)
1969 - Traded to New Orleans (for Gary Cuozzo)
1970 - John Ward, T, Oklahoma State
1971 - Leo Hayden, RB, Ohio State
1972 a- Jeff Siemon, LB, Stanford (choice from New England)
       b- Traded to N.Y. Giants (for Fran Tarkenton)
1973 - Chuck Foreman, RB, Miami (Fla)
1974 a- Fred McNeill, LB, UCLA (choice from Atlanta)
       b- Steve Riley, T, USC
1975 - Mark Mullaney, DE, Colorado State
1976 - James White, DT, Oklahoma State
1977 - Tommy Kramer, QB, Rice
1978 - Randy Holloway, DE, Pittsburgh
1979 - Ted Brown, HB, North Carolina State
1980 - Doug Martin, DT, Washington
1981 - Traded to Baltimore for two 2nd round picks in 1982

HUNDRED YARD RUSHERS

In the 21-year history of the Minnesota Vikings only 10 different players have rushed for 100 or more yards in a single game. Chuck Foreman had 17 100-yard games from 1973-1978.

HUNDRED YARD RUSHING GAMES

Date	Player	Opponent	ATT	YARDS
Dec. 3, 1961	Raymond Hayes	vs Los Angeles	18	123
Dec. 17, 1961	Mel Triplett	vs Chicago	15	121
Dec. 9, 1962	Tommy Mason	vs Detroit	16	138
Dec. 16, 1962	Tommy Mason	vs Baltimore	20	143
Nov. 17, 1963	Tommy Mason	vs Baltimore	12	146
Sept. 13, 1964	Tommy Mason	vs Baltimore	20	137
Sept. 13, 1964	Bill Brown	vs Baltimore	20	103
Oct. 18, 1964	Tommy Mason	vs Pittsburgh	14	124
Nov. 15, 1964	Bill Brown	vs Baltimore	19	106
Dec. 6, 1964	Bill Brown	vs NY Giants	18	103
Oct. 17, 1965	Bill Brown	vs Chicago	15	117
Oct. 31, 1965	Bill Brown	vs Cleveland	26	138
Dec. 5, 1965	Tommy Mason	vs Green Bay	21	101
Sept. 25, 1966	Bill Brown	vs Dallas	20	115
Dec. 18, 1966	Dave Osborn	vs Chicago	19	118
Oct. 29, 1967	Dave Osborn	vs Atlanta	22	103
Nov. 5, 1967	Dave Osborn	vs NY Giants	16	115
Dec. 3, 1967	Dave Osborn	vs Green Bay	21	155
Sept. 14, 1968	Clinton Jones	vs Atlanta	17	101
Sept. 29, 1968	Bill Brown	vs Chicago	12	109
Oct. 12, 1969	Dave Osborn	vs Chicago	15	106
Dec. 5, 1970	Dave Osborn	vs Chicago	29	139
Nov. 28, 1971	Clinton Jones	vs Atlanta	22	155
Nov. 12, 1972	Oscar Reed	vs Detroit	23	124
Sept. 23, 1973	Chuck Foreman	vs Chicago	16	116
Oct. 7, 1973	Chuck Foreman	vs Detroit	16	114
Nov. 11, 1973	Bill Brown	vs Detroit	19	101
Dec. 8, 1973	Chuck Foreman	vs Green Bay	19	100
Oct. 19, 1975	Chuck Foreman	vs Detroit	22	107
Oct. 27, 1975	Chuck Foreman	vs Chicago	26	102
Nov. 9, 1975	Chuck Foreman	vs Atlanta	26	102
Nov. 16, 1975	Chuck Foreman	vs New Orleans	24	117
Nov. 23, 1975	Chuck Foreman	vs San Diego	33	127
Oct. 4, 1976	Chuck Foreman	vs Pittsburgh	27	148
Oct. 24, 1976	Chuck Foreman	vs Philadelphia	28	200*
Nov. 14, 1976	Chuck Foreman	vs Seattle	17	100
Oct. 16, 1977	Chuck Foreman	vs Chicago	26	150
Nov. 13, 1977	Chuck Foreman	vs Cincinnati	29	133
Nov. 27, 1977	Chuck Foreman	vs Green Bay	26	101
Dec. 17, 1977	Chuck Foreman	vs Detroit	33	156
Sept. 3, 1978	Chuck Foreman	vs New Orleans	18	122
Oct. 26, 1978	Chuck Foreman	vs Dallas	22	101
Oct. 12, 1980	Ted Brown	vs Chicago	22	113
Sept. 27, 1981	Ted Brown	vs Green Bay	31	129
Nov. 8, 1981	Ted Brown	vs Tampa Bay	21	109
Nov. 23, 1981	Ted Brown	vs Atlanta	16	108

*Viking single game record.

VIKING LEADERS, YEAR-BY-YEAR

	PASSING	Att-Comp-Yds	RUSHING	Att-Yds	RECEIVING	No. Yds.
1961	Tarkenton	280-157-1997	McElhenny	120-570	Reichow	50-859
1962	Tarkenton	329-163-2595	Mason	167-740	Reichow	39-561
1963	Tarkenton	297-170-2311	Mason	166-763	Flatley	51-867
1964	Tarkenton	306-171-2506	Brown	226-866	Brown	48-703
1965	Tarkenton	329-171-2609	Brown	160-699	Flatley	50-896
1966	Tarkenton	358-192-2561	Brown	251-829	Flatley	50-777
1967	Kapp	214-102-1386	Osborn	215-972	Osborn	34-282
1968	Kapp	248-129-1699	Brown	222-805	Washington	46-756
1969	Kapp	237-120-1726	Osborn	186-643	Washington	39-821
1970	Cuozzo	257-128-1720	Osborn	207-681	Washington	44-702
1971	Cuozzo	168- 75- 842	Jones	180-675	Grim	45-691
1972	Tarkenton	378-215-2651	Reed	151-639	Gilliam	47-1035
1973	Tarkenton	274-169-2113	Foreman	182-801	Gilliam	42-907
1974	Tarkenton	351-199-2598	Foreman	199-777	Foreman	53-586
1975	Tarkenton	425-273-2994	Foreman	280-1070	Foreman	73-691
1976	Tarkenton	412-255-2961	Foreman	278-1155	Foreman	55-567
1977	Tarkenton	258-155-1734	Foreman	270-1112	Rashad	51-681
1978	Tarkenton	572-345-3468	Foreman	237-749	Young	88-704
1979	Kramer	566-315-3397	Young	188-708	Rashad	80-1156
1980	Kramer	522-299-3582	Brown	219-912	Rashad	69-1095
1981	Kramer	593-322-3912	Brown	274-1063	Brown	83-694

	INTERCEPTIONS	No.	SCORING	Pts.	PUNTING	No. Avg.
1961	Hawkins	5	Reichow	66	Mercer	63-39.0
1962	Sharockman	6	Christopherson	61	Mercer	19-43.5
1963	Sharockman	5	Cox	75	Cox	70-38.7
1964	Rose	6	Cox	103	Walden	72-46.4
1965	Sharockman	6	Cox	113	Walden	51-42.1
1966	Hackbart	5	Cox	88	Walden	60-41.1
1967	Mackbee	5	Cox	77	Walden	75-41.6
1968	Krause	7	Cox	88	Hill	33-41.0
1969	Bryant	8	Cox	121	Lee	67-40.0
1970	Sharockman	7	Cox	125	McNeill	61-38.0
1971	West	7	Cox	91	Lee	89-39.5
1972	Krause	6	Cox	97	Eischeid	62-42.7
1973	Bryant	7	Cox	96	Eischeid	66-39.8
1974	N. Wright	6	Foreman	90	Eischeid	73-36.1
1975	Krause	10	Foreman	132	Clabo	73-41.1
1976	N. Wright	7	Cox	89	Clabo	69-38.8
1977	Bryant	4	S. White, Foreman	54	Clabo	83-39.8
1978	Bryant	7	Danmeier	72	Coleman	51-39.0
1979	Hannon, N. Wright	4	Danmeier	66	Coleman	90-39.5
1980	Turner	6	Danmeier	81	Coleman	81-38.8
1981	Hannon, Teal	4	Danmeier	97	Coleman	88-41.4

BUD WHO?

Through the years, sports fans in this part of the country have had fewer nicknames applied to their favorite players than in many other areas. There have, however, been some notable exceptions. Can you match the following persons with their real first names?

1. Bud Grant
2. Rip Hawkins
3. Pug Lund
4. Billy Martin
5. Bronko Nagurski
6. Tony Oliva
7. Shorty Pleis
8. Bombo Rivera
9. Duck Shifflett
10. Bud Wilkinson
11. Butch Wynegar

a. Alfred
b. Bill
c. Bronislaw
d. Charles
e. Francis
f. Garland
g. Harold
h. Harry
i. Jesus
j. Pedro
k. Ross

Answers: 1h; 2k; 3e; 4a; 5c; 6j; 7b; 8i; 9f; 10c; 11g.

Gopher Football: A Century of Thrills

by DAVE MONA

The University of Minnesota celebrated the completion of 100 years of football during the 1981 season.

The first recorded intercollegiate game between Minnesota and another college took place on Sept. 29, 1882, when Minnesota defeated nearby Hamline 4-0 at the Minnesota State Fairgrounds.

A year later the Gophers found their first coach, Prof. Thomas Peebles, whose team compiled a 1-2 record.

In 1885 Alf Pillsbury joined the Minnesota team and played there for the next eight years in an era not marked by strict NCAA regulation. In 1890 the Gophers played their first out-of-state competition, taking on Grinnell College of Iowa and the University of Wisconsin.

The University of Iowa joined the schedule in 1891, and Michigan and Northwestern became regular opponents the next year.

The battle for the Little Brown Jug is part of the annual Minnesota-Michigan rivalry.

At the turn of the century, Dr. Henry Williams became Minnesota's first full-time, salaried football coach, a position he held for 21 seasons.

Memorial Stadium was built in 1924, the final year for the Gophers under Williams' successor, Bill Spaulding. Dr. Clarence Speers took over from Spaulding in 1925 and lasted four years. That period was highlighted by the play of Bronko Nagurski, an All-America performer at both tackle and fullback.

Gopher football reached its greatest heights in the 1930s under Coach Bernie Bierman. In the decade from 1932 to 1941 the Gophers won six Big Ten championships, five national championships and had five undefeated seasons. During those years they won 63 games against just 12 losses and five ties.

Minnesota players dominated the All-America selections under Bierman. The 1934 team, still picked by many as one of the all-time great college football teams, featured three All-Americans: halfback Francis (Pug) Lund, end Frank (Butch) Larson, and guard Bill Bevan. The next season saw tackle Dick Smith and guard Bud Wilkinson chosen to several All-America teams. In 1936 it was tackle Ed Widseth and halfback Andy Uram.

Ray King made it at end in 1937, and Francis Twedell at guard in 1938. Halfback George Franck and tackle Urban

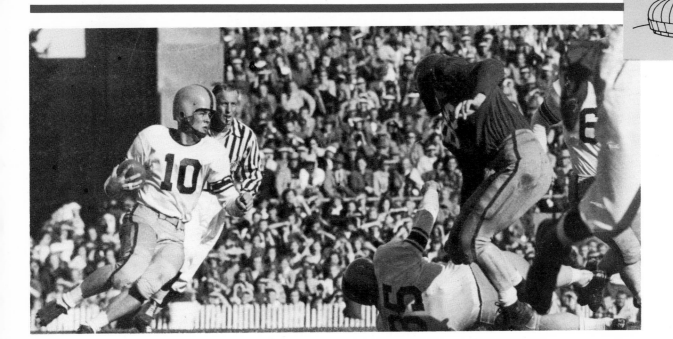

Odson were picked from the 1940 National Champions, and Bruce Smith, a halfback and Minnesota's only Heisman Trophy winner, was a 1941 All-American. Dick Wildung, a tackle, was chosen in 1942, while Leo Nomellini was an All-America tackle in 1948 and 1949, and Clayton Tonnemaker was the center on the 1949 team.

Bierman resigned after his 1950 team finished 1-7-1. He was replaced by former Ohio State All-American Wes Fesler, whose teams were 10-13-4 over the next three years.

The highlight of the Fesler years was the play of Winona's Paul Giel, who won the Chicago *Tribune*'s Big Ten Most Valuable Player Award in both 1952 and 1953, and who finished second to Notre Dame's Johnny Lattner in the Heisman Trophy voting.

Joining Giel in the Gopher backfield were Bob McNamara, a 1954 All-America selection, and Gino Capelletti, later an All-Pro wide receiver and kicker. When Fesler left he was replaced by Murray Warmath, whose 18-year career as head coach was the second longest in Gopher history.

Warmath was unknown locally when he took the job, and, in the late 1950s was the victim of a vicious "dump Murray" campaign that saw garbage thrown on the lawn of his suburban home.

In 1960, however, he was named National Coach of the Year with the first of his two Rose Bowl teams. That squad lost to an underdog Washington team, but the next year the team defeated UCLA for Minnesota's only Rose Bowl victory.

Warmath's teams were the first to feature black players recruited from eastern and southern states—players such as Sandy Stephens, Bobby Bell, Carl Eller and Judge Dickson. Warmath's teams compiled an 86-77-7 record over the years and gave Minnesota its most recent share of a Big Ten title in 1967.

Cal Stoll, a Minnesota graduate, took over from Warmath in 1972. In seven years under Stoll the Gophers won 39 and lost 38.

Stoll's successor was one-time Gopher quarterback Joe Salem, whose teams were 15-17-1 from 1979 through 1981.

Top: Paul Giel was a two-time All-America halfback and runner-up in the Heisman Trophy balloting in 1953. Bottom: Bud Grant played end for the late Bernie Bierman and was named the Gophers' most valuable player in 1949. He went on to play both pro football and basketball.

Bert Baston 1915-16 E

Bobby Lee Bell 1961-62 T

Bill Bevan 1934 G

Aaron Brown 1965 E

Tom Brown 1960 G

Bill Daley 1943 FB

Carl Eller 1963 T

George Franck 1940 HB

Paul Giel 1952-53 HB

Kenneth Haycraft 1928 E

Bob Hobert 1956 T

Herb Joesting 1926-27 FB

Doug Kingsriter 1971 E

Francis (Pug) Lund 1934 HB

Earl Martineau 1923 HB

John McGovern 1909 QB

Bob McNamara 1954 FB, HB

Clarence (Biggie) Munn 1931 G

Leo Nomellini 1948-49 T, G

Bronko Nagurski 1929 T

Bruce Smith 1941 HB

Dick Smith 1935 T

Bob Stein 1967 E

Sandy Stephens 1961 QB

Clayton Tonnemaker 1949 C

Ed Widseth 1936 T

Dick Wildung 1941-42 T

Bud Wilkinson 1935 G

Gopher All-Americans not pictured: Tom Brown 1960 G; George Gibson, 1928 G; Harold Hanson, 1927 G; Herb Hein, 1943 E; Ray King, 1937 E; Frank Larson, 1933-34 E; C.I. (Shorty) Long, 1916 QB; Urban Odson, 1940 T; Francis Twedell, 1938 G; James Walker, 1910 T.

Metropolitan Sports Facilities Commission

Dan Brutger,
Chairman

Donald Poss,
Executive Director

Jerry Bell,
Administrative Assistant

Dennis Alfton,
Assistant to Executive Director

Left to right: Richard Radman, treasurer; Jerry Bell, administrative assistant; Donald Poss, executive director; Solveig Premack, commissioner; Ron Gornick, vice chairman; Marion Kennon, secretary; Josephine Nunn, commissioner. Not pictured are Dan Brutger, chairman, and Kelly Gage, commissioner.

Metrodome Contractors

Acoustical Tile
Dale Tile Company
Minneapolis, MN

Asphalt Paving
Bituminous Roadways, Inc.
Minneapolis, MN

Balance Doors
Ellison Bronze Company
Falconer, NY

Bollards
Linders Fabricating &
   Manufacturing, Inc.
St. Paul, MN

Metal Rails & Bus Gates
Iron Works, Inc.
Hopkins, MN

Caissons
Kirkman Foundation Company
Lakeville, MN

Carpentry
C. F. Haglin & Sons Co., Inc.
Minneapolis, MN

Carpet
DVR&W, Inc.
Minneapolis, MN

Ceramic Tile
Twin City Tile & Marble Co.
Minneapolis, MN

Chair Seating
American Seating Company
Grand Rapids, Mich.

Concessions Deck Coating
Twin Ports Seal Systems, Inc.
Duluth, MN

Concessions Electrical
Riser-Kvalsten Electric
St. Paul, MN

Concessions Mechanical
Axel Newman Heating &
   Plumbing
St. Paul, MN

Concessions Millwork
C. F. Haglin & Sons Company
Minneapolis, MN

Concessions Painting
Casci Decorators, Inc.
Roseville, MN

Concessions Rolling Doors
Door Systems Inc.
Minneapolis, MN

Concrete Pavement
Concrete Curb Company
Burnsville, MN

Dampproofing
Twin Ports Seal Systems, Inc.
Duluth, MN

Electrical
Sterling Electric Construction
Minneapolis, MN

Elevators
S & N Elevator Company
St. Paul, MN

Excavation
Ames Construction, Inc.
Burnsville, MN

Finish Hardware
Bredemus Hardware Company
St. Paul, MN

Fire Protection
Northstar Fire Protection Co.
St. Paul, MN

Flagpoles
Specialty Sales Service, Inc.
Minneapolis, MN

General Mechanical
Hayes Contractors, Inc.
Minneapolis, MN

Glass & Glazing
Hoffer's, Inc.
Minneapolis, MN

Graphics
Leroy Signs, Inc.
Minneapolis, MN

Gypsum Drywall
Minuti-Ogle, Inc. and
   Leverette, Weekes & Co.
A Joint Venture
Minneapolis, MN

Hollow Metal Doors & Frames
American Steel Products Co.
Farmingdale, NY

Insulation
Wells Engineering
Minneapolis, MN

Metal Deck
Northern States Steel
   Builders, Inc.
Duluth, MN

Metal Lockers
Hauenstein & Burmeister
Minneapolis, MN

Metal Wall Panels
Northern States Steel
   Builders, Inc.
Duluth, MN

Miscellaneous Iron
C. W. Olson, Inc.
Minneapolis, MN

Overhead Sectional Doors
Door Systems, Inc.
Minneapolis, MN

Painting
Schletty-McCann Painting
St. Paul, MN

Pre-Cast Concrete
Spancrete Midwest, Inc.
Osseo, MN

Poured-In-Place Concrete
Knutson Construction Co.
Minneapolis, MN

Retaining Wall
Knutson Construction Co.
Minneapolis, MN

Retractable Seating Supports
Rollway Grandstand Corp.
Los Angeles, Calif.

Revolving Doors
International Steel Company
Evansville, Ind.

Rolling Doors
Pearson & LaLonde, Inc.
Minneapolis, MN

Roof Fabric & Cable
Birdair Structures, Inc.
Buffalo, NY

**Roof Ring Cast-In-Place
Concrete**
Adolfson & Peterson, Inc.
Minneapolis, MN

Roof Ring Pre-Cast Concrete
Bladholm Brothers Culvert Co.
Osseo, MN

Roof Ring Structural Steel
Crown Iron Works Company
Minneapolis, MN

Sealants & Fillers
Right-Way Caulking, Inc.
Anoka, MN

Site Utilities
Axel Newman, Inc.
St. Paul, MN

Sod
Minnesota Valley Landscape
Bloomington, MN

Synthetic Turf
Superturf, Inc.
Garland, TX

Ticket Booths
Don Harstad Company
Fridley, MN

Toilet Accessories
Specialty Sales Service, Inc.
Minneapolis, MN

Toilet Partitions
Builders Engineering Co.
St. Paul, MN

Trees & Grates
Minnesota Valley Landscape
Bloomington, MN

Vikings' Acoustical Ceiling
Ceilings, Inc.
Champlin, MN

Vikings' Carpentry
Rocon Construction Company
St. Paul, MN

Vikings' Ceramic Tile
Twin City Tile & Marble Co.
Minneapolis, MN

Vikings' Electrical
Riser/Kvalsten Electric Co.
St. Paul, MN

Vikings' Fire Protection
Northstar Fire Protection Co.
St. Paul, MN

Vikings' Gypsum Drywall
Minuti-Ogle, Inc. and Leverette,
   Weekes & Co.
A Joint Venture
Minneapolis, MN

**Vikings' Hollow Metal Doors
& Frames**
Bredemus Hardware Company
St. Paul, MN

Vikings' Masonry
Axel H. Ohman, Inc.
Minneapolis, MN

Vikings' Mechanical
Hayes Contractors, Inc.
Minneapolis, MN

Vikings' Miscellaneous Iron
Linders Fabricating & Mfg.
St. Paul, MN

**Vikings' Paint & Vinyl Wall
Covering**
Schletty-McCann Painting, Inc.
St. Paul, MN

Vikings' Private Box Glass
Hoffer's, Inc.
Minneapolis, MN

Vikings' Resilient Flooring
Ebony Interiors, Inc.
Minneapolis, MN

Vikings' Toilet Accessories
Specialty Sales Service, Inc.
Minneapolis, MN

Waste Handling System
Compaction Services Co.
Minneapolis, MN

Waterproofing
Nichols & Hines, Inc.
St. Paul, MN

Acknowledgments

The building of the Hubert H. Humphrey Metrodome has been marked by controversy. From a strictly bricks and mortar standpoint, the construction was remarkable compared with that of other large public buildings in other parts of the country. The Metrodome was finished on time and under budget.

Most of the criticism of the project was not much on the building itself, but on the way it was delivered to the public as a fait accompli.

Critics argued that it would benefit only the rich, that the public had little or no choice in the process, and that baseball especially was meant to be played under the open air.

Perhaps the true test of the Metrodome will be to come back in 1992 to see what people think of it then. The skyway system linking downtown Minneapolis buildings was not universally cheered when it was suggested, but today the skyway system has few detractors.

Despite the controversy surrounding the stadium, it was relatively easy to convince some of the best writers in the area to contribute sections to this book. Joe Soucheray, never a fan of the Metrodome, agreed to contribute a section on Met Stadium. Pat Reusse, a frequent Metrodome critic on the St. Paul newspapers, salved his conscience when his research revealed that the idea for the dome may have originated in St. Paul.

I should thank Brian Anderson, Maureen Ryan and the staff of MSP Publications for their technical assistance in putting the book together. Joe O'Connell, a long-time friend, put in countless hours rummaging through photo files on our behalf. The Twins, Vikings and Gopher public relations and sports information departments returned literally dozens of phone calls and spent hours checking facts for the historical sections of the book.

We are also indebted to Larry Loeschen for allowing us to reproduce the Halsey Hall series of baseball cards. Marc Hequet gave up part of his Christmas holidays to write the section on the actual building of the Metrodome.

The Metrodome staff, and Jerry Bell in particular, were most cooperative in the compiling of this book, and Muriel Humphrey Brown enthusiastically contributed a beautiful and touching foreword.

In addition, Jim Klobuchar was willing to recall again the frenetic conception of the Minnesota Vikings. Scott Papillon contributed a year-by-year section with the Vikings, and Bill Morlock and Rick Little, co-authors of *Split Doubleheader*, put together a history of the Minnesota Twins. Chuck Benda came through with a history of Memorial Stadium in the expectation that the Gophers someday would play in the Metrodome. Charles Johnson, one of the people who brought major league baseball to Minnesota, summarized those efforts, and Calvin Griffith took time out from his schedule to recall what was going through his mind the day he suggested moving the Washington Senators to Minnesota. In every case, the writers and interviewees gave up their time with very little urging.

And finally, I'd like to thank my wife, Linda, and my sons, Kirk and Erik, who became used to my leaving home for several hours on most fall weekends to meet the deadlines for this book.

David Mona is president of David L. Mona & Associates, a Minneapolis-based public relations firm. A Minneapolis native, he was a vendor at Metropolitan Stadium when it was built in 1956. He attended baseball games at Nicollet Park as a child with his father, Lute Mona, the former basketball and baseball coach at Minneapolis South High School.

Dave Mona attended the University of Minnesota, graduating with a degree in journalism. He was sports editor of the Minnesota *Daily* and the Minnesota Gopher yearbook. He was a reporter for WCCO TV, and, from 1965 through 1969, was a reporter for the Minneapolis *Tribune*. In 1968 and 1969 he covered the Minnesota Twins for the *Tribune*.

He has been a regular columnist for MPLS.ST.PAUL Magazine since the first issue of that publication over 10 years ago. He now writes the Sports Mailbag column for MPLS.ST.PAUL and co-hosts a Sunday morning sports talk show on WCCO Radio with Minneapolis *Tribune* sports columnist Sid Hartman.

1981 Minnesota Twins

Top Row: Jim Wiesner, visitors' clubhouse; Gary Ward, lf; Pete Redfern, p; Jerry Koosman, p; Rob Wilfong, 2b; Jack O'Connor, p; John Verhoeven, p; Al Williams, p; Roger Erickson, p; Dave Engle, rf; Roy Smalley, ss; Dick Martin, trainer.

Middle Row: Ron Jackson, 1b; Pete Mackanin, 2b; Danny Goodwin, 1b; Hosken Powell, rf; Fernando Arroyo, p; Mickey Hatcher, cf; Ray Smith, c; Doug Corbett, p; Rick Sofield, lf; Don Cooper, p; Butch Wynegar, c.

Front Row: Ray Crump, equipment; Chuck Baker, ss; Sal Butera, c; Glenn Adams, dh; Johnny Podres, coach; Billy Gardner, coach; Johnny Goryl, manager; Rick Stelmaszek, coach; Karl Kuehl, coach; Greg Johnston, cf; John Castino, 3b; Jim Dunn, clubhouse.

Batboys: Dan O'Hara, Jeff Jennings, Mark Stavros, Tark Ericksen.

Autographs